The Healing Power Within

The Story of Natural Healing and Cellular Energy

by Dr. Jack Tips

For information:

Apple-A-Day Press
3736 Bee Caves Road, Suite 1-174
Austin, Texas 78746

512.328.3996

ISBN 0-929167-34-1

Library of Congress Cataloging-in-Publication Data

Tips, Jack C.

The Healing Power Within; non-fiction, clinical nutrition / Jack Tips

p. cm.

ISBN 0-929167-34-1

1. Diet—Health aspects
2. Diet—Physiological aspects
3. Diet Therapy—Physiological aspects
4. Food—Health aspects
5. Nutrition—Health aspects
6. Nutritionally-induced diseases
7. α-glycopeptides I. Title

Second Edition

Typesetting, Lay Out: Keith Bahlmann, Bahl Graphics, Austin, Texas
Proofreading: Judy Woodrow San Rafael, CA / Joanne McRae Schultz / Saskatoon, Canada, Janine Tips / Austin, Texas
Indexing: Keith Bahlmann, Bahl Graphics, Austin, Texas
Cover Design: Don Crawford, Austin, Texas
Typing: Jessica Johnson, Austin, Texas
Printed: United States of America

The Healing Power Within
The Story of Natural Healing and Cellular Energy

by Dr. Jack Tips

For more information about supplementation with α-glycopeptides
(polysaccharide/polypeptides), please contact:

Dedications

First and foremost, this book is dedicated to Russ Hall—a man of vision, heart, and wisdom—who brought alpha-glycopeptides to the world market so that virtually anyone and everyone has the opportunity to improve their health in order to live a full and varied life.

To my fellow clinicians who understand how α-glycopeptides fill a most critical niche in the true healing paradigm, and have the dedication to implement this information for the benefit of those who trust their judgment.

To all the people, the world over, who improve their health by consistent supplementation of α-glycopeptides. Health is won or lost day by day, cell by cell. I salute your winning spirit.

Benediction

Thanks and praise to Universal Love — the Sound and Light that leads us to Truth. May we heed the message that our inward listening ears and inward seeing eyes reveal.

Foreword by the Author

This book is written for everyone who is interested in learning more about how nutrition serves their body's ability to maintain the best of health. It is particularly written for natural health clinicians because they are in the front ranks of healing, and in desperate need of tools that help unleash the body's innate healing processes, despite the impediments of the environment, food supply, and lifestyles.

For You. Most importantly, this book endeavors to teach the pathways that everyone's body must traverse to experience that "I feel terrific!" level of health, despite the challenges of life in the 21st Century. The necessary biochemistry and biology discussions are soon followed by simple summary explanations. If you are not particularly interested in reading about molecules (and I can certainly understand that), you can "cut to the chase" and grab the salient points by scanning ahead to the summaries along the way.

Yet some shoptalk can't be avoided. A discussion at this level will take us into some technical information. I've done my best to keep this information simple and easy to understand, but it's inevitable that I must delve a wee bit into biochemistry to make the points about how α-glycopeptides (polysaccharides/polypeptides) support cellular energy and cellular signaling (communication with the immune system). It's fun to learn about how our bodies work and how to promote health and longevity. So I hope you agree on reading this material.

It seems that everyone is looking for something that makes them feel better and prevents their bodies from getting old and acquiring diseases. Rightly so. I've always believed in starting each day with a terrific nutritional boost. Then the day can unfold as best it can, and if it's less than optimal, at least the body's basic nutrition is already in place.

I like that philosophy—it's easy. It's founded on what our mothers told us time and again, "Breakfast is the most important meal of the day." If we respect our bodies and their nutritional needs at the start of each day, then the day can unfold without remorse. And each morning brings renewal.

For the past nine months, I have started each day with a couple of teaspoons of an α-glycopeptides product (called PXP® for polysaccharides/polypeptides) along with one capsule of the HFi (humate) product. Later I follow this with an array of greens, raw organic vegetable juice, and the supplements that I want to include for whatever I'm into at the time. After all that, I say, "Let come what may. Go with the flow of the day," and try not to misbehave too much with all the Texas barbecue, Tex-Mex food, and gourmet chocolates that abound here in Austin."

My dear friend and mentor (Don Ginn, whom I met over 40 years ago) introduced me to *nutritional, alpha polysaccharide/polypeptides*, henceforth referred to as α-*glycopeptides* for simplicity—the subject of this book. With a healthy degree of skepticism (we all need to think for ourselves and gather our own experiences), I committed to a 30-day trial.

Why would I be skeptical? Well, being a natural health practitioner (clinical nutritionist, classical homeopath, herbalist) who lives a fairly natural health lifestyle, I'm in excellent health. I just did not think that I had much room to improve (except of course in my personality, relationships, communications, and understanding of Life.) Further, the concept of the product sounded so absolutely fabulous, I figured that, like other highly touted specialty products, they all seem to work for someone else, but not for me.

Was I surprised! By the end of the trial month, I ordered a triple supply and started taking a larger dose. This was an exception to the errant concept: "If a little is good then more must be better," and in this case, more was actually better and I was thrilled with the results I was experiencing. Evidently, I had a lot of cells that could use some more energy.

In fact, I was ecstatic about the overall well-being I was feeling – more energy, better sleep, sharper mind, more internal calm, and more fundamental, innate joy in living. My already great health just shifted into a noticeably better and vibrant dimension. The "lights" just got a little brighter. I was impressed to say the least, and so grateful for what α-glycopeptide supplementation was doing for my already fine quality of life—always room for improvements!

I felt so blessed by these life enhancements, but next I needed to know if the product would work for others. Over six weeks, I recommended the product to 164 people and collected statistics at the 30 and 60-day marks.

After 30-60 days on α-glycopeptides, out of 164 people, how many:

- Liked, even loved, the taste? 163 (Only my dear former clinic manager thought it was yucky and would not consider taking it – just goes to show, eh? A prophet isn't known in his own land!)

- Liked it enough to write a glowing testimonial? 58 (Unfortunately, I can't share most of them with you due to new USA laws about expressing health benefits, but know this—there are some doozies, incredible changes, much to my great joy!)

- Wanted to try it for another month? 159

- Wanted to get the large jar to hasten the benefits? 92

- Felt some form of adjustment (detox) reaction? 8 (possibly 9). Not a bad thing and showed the efficacy of the improvement trend.

- Reported energy improvements? 121

- Reported mental clarity improvements? 71

- Reported improvement in sleep? 17

- Reported an improving trend in a primary health concern? 158

- Referred friends to take the product? 19

- Wanted an extra jar for a family member? 33

- Showed improvement in their doctors' lab reports after 60 days? 32 (The two that did not show improvements did not show any deterioration.)

- With elevated cholesterol improved in 60 days? 27 out of 28.

- With documented elevated homocysteine (heart health marker) levels showed improvement in 60 days? 18 out of 18.

- With elevated A1C (glycosylated hemoglobin A1C—a glucose control marker), how many improved in 60 days? (also worked with diet and excercise) 14 out of 14

Six weeks is a short period of time, reporting a small segment of people, and a unique demographic, yet the statistics are glowingly positive. After only a short time, I realized that the inclusion of α-glycopeptides into anyone's diet would be most advantageous. Please note that my statistics are not considered a "blind" study because inevitably people embrace other lifestyle changes when consulting with me. But be assured of this, before using α-glycopeptides, my statistics while good, were not as good. α-Glycopeptides have most certainly improved people's outcomes beyond what other natural health therapies were previously accomplishing. That's the point!

α-Glycopeptides seem to put people on the fast track for health improvements. Here's what clinicians are saying about why they like it:

- **Hypoallergenic** – 99.9% of people tolerate α-glycopeptides, (My opinion). Even people who are allergic to table rice are using α-glycopeptides without adverse reactions.

- **Cost effective** – People know they are being cost effective when their improves energy.

- **Tasty** – Practically everyone likes the taste (except the one aforementioned).

- **Good Compliance** – Very little attrition, practically everyone stays with it. Easy to take a teaspoon upon arising, and that's it!

- **No Contraindications** – The product is not contraindicated for any prescription medications, or health concerns.

- **It works!** – Most people know it's helping them, and that makes clinicians happy.

- **Cellular ATP energy production** – The optimal fuel for the mitochondria. Sets the stage for the body to heal itself by fueling the necessary energy improvements.

- **Cell-Signaling** – Supports the glycopeptides and glycolipids used in proper cellular communication. Nutrition for people with autoimmune and chronic degenerative, inflammatory concerns. Supports the body's anti-inflammatory processes.

- **Bio-Ready (assimilable)** – 99.99% uptake. The 'alpha' size means rapid absorption into the mitocondria of the cells, even for people with impaired digestion. This is called *cellular bioavailability*. Further, α-glycopeptides do not need to be "actively transported[§]" through the cell membranes, so there is not an expenditure of ATP (the body's life energy) in order to derive the benefits.

- **Completely natural, pesticide free, non-contaminated source** – Straight from remote Nature, through the grinder and into the hopper (hydrolyser), then into the jar. A "whole food" product.

- **Enhances nutritional programs** – Doctor's report that healthy cells become more receptive to the beneficial aspects of vitamins, minerals, herbs, homeopathics, and nutriments.

- **Anti-inflammatory assistance** – The anthocyanins and proanthocyanins that accompany the α-glycopeptides are anti-oxidants that work both inside and outside the cells and support the cell membranes to reduce inflammations that ultimately lead to aging, altered tissue function, weak immunity, and free-radical pathologies.

- **Anti-aging** – Supports DNA and RNA repair via the nucleic acid configurations within the cells. Reduces inflammation and free radical damage. When cells reproduce, the new cells can be healthier.

- **Rich in nutrients** – Antioxidants, essential-proteins, anthocyanins and proanthocyanins, bioflavanoids, healing sugars, essential lipids, and trace minerals abound.

- **Helps the body relieve cellular hormonal resistance** – Allow the neuroendocrine system to function with greater precision.

- **Gentle detoxification** – Engergizes the body's innate detoxification of acquired toxins as well as metabolic wastes.

- **Helps build the body's alkaline reserve** – Helps counter metabolic acidosis and supports calcium metabolism.

- **Energy to heal** – First our cells must take care of cellular business. Then, if there is energy left over, the cells can repair their DNA. When the cells heal, the body heals itself. Since natural health professionals are engaged in the art and science of helping the body heal itself, increasing cellular energy is both a commonsensical and essential practice.

With benefits like these, I do feel a strong obligation to let others know about this amazing life enhancer. My personal dream is to have a million people benefit from α-glycopeptides within the next 5 years as a result of this information. Let's learn about what I believe is a tremendous advantage for humanity that's arrived at a time when we so desperately need it. Blessings,

Jack Tips, N.D, Ph.D., C.Hom., C.C.N.[1]

---

1   N.D. Doctorate Degree in Naturopathy (American Naturopathic Medical Association) / Ph.D. Clinical Nutrition, Dr. Roger Williams School of Nutrition Science, Clayton, MO / C.Hom. Certificate Classical Homeopathy, Hahnemann Academy of North America / C.C.N. Certified Clinical Nutritionist, International & American Associations of Clinical Nutritionists / Licensed in NY.

Disclaimer

This book discusses the nature, role and effect of α-glycopeptides as a whole-body nutritional supplement. Many people are finding that the inclusion of α-glycopeptides into their diets have profound benefits for their well-being. Many understand that true healing is of the spirit and the body's sacred covenant with Life itself, and that no one— no institution, no science, no practice, no person, no profession, no medicine—can claim to be doing the healing or own the rights to, or monopolize, "healing," lest they usurp the body's God-given innate intelligence. Such an act demonstrates blatant ignorance of Natural Law.

This book does not diagnose. It does not consult with anyone about anything. It does not prescribe. It does not treat any disease whatsoever. It does not make any curative claims, nor does it make claims for α-glycopeptide supplementation except as whole body nutrition. It presents information for educational and information purposes only. If a reader is interested in diseases and the suppression of disease symptoms, please seek the advice of a qualified medical professional before making use of any of this information. If the reader is interested in natural health, please seek the advice of a qualified natural health professional. This book is the opinion of the author, and not the opinion of the Enzacta Corporation, maker of the unique proprietary α-glycopeptides discussed in these pages.

Author's Disclosure

Since becoming aware of the α-glycopeptides products on the market, I began a year of due diligence that included: 1) personal use, 2) recommendations to hundreds of people to try α-glycopeptides so I could learn from their personal experiences, 3) meetings with the chief plant-geneticist and the manufacturing director, 4) personal conferences with the founder, and 5) meeting with principle corporate personnel and key field distributors. These efforts have resulted in my belief that: 1) α-glycopeptides are a bona fide valuable nutritional supplement that can enhance virtually everyone's well being, 2) the manufacturing/ marketing company is comprised of honorable, honest, dedicated people, 3) association with such dedicated scientists, business people, and marketers is a good thing, and 4) affiliation with the corporate agenda to reach millions of people with the benefits of α-glycopeptides is a worthwhile and ethical endeavor.

Thus, I have become an independent member of the marketing corporation. I have no affiliation with the corporate office and am just another guy in the field disseminating information. I have not been hired by the company to write this material, nor does it represent any labeling for their product. I wrote this solely as a personal labor of love. I would like to disclose to you here at the onset that I am delighted to be affiliated with those who share this information, both those who went before me and those who join after me.

Thus, please know that I have a small degree of a vested interest in this material as I have freely chosen to participate as a rank-and-file independent representative, in the marketing program provided by the company. I feel strongly that finally someone's doing it right, respect for Nature's healing food and the natural laws of life, wise and judicious application of science, integrity in manufacturing, fairness and honesty in marketing. I believe this in its entirety, is the "real deal." To the very best of my understanding, I can say this to you: "May the blessings be."

Helpful Hints

The § symbol. In telling this story, I must use some terminology from science and the natural health disciplines. Certain words are denoted with a superscript § symbol to let you know that the word is defined in the glossary at the back of this book. Some words have special definitions from the natural health perspective. Words that connote a meaning that is different from common usage are also designated with "§".

Summary Boxes. If you were to think, "I don't want to read about all the metabolic pathways this guy is talking about," all you need to do is skip ahead and go to the "Summary Box" for a quick overview of prior discussions.

So let's get started on this adventure of a lifetime.

Contents

Introduction to Universal "Miracle Molecules" for Health

Welcome to what I expect will soon be a tremendous blessing for your health and your life. It is such a great pleasure to share with you what is so much more than just another major milestone in the quest for better health—it's the single most important array of nutritional molecules available on the earth today!

I know. That's a bold statement, yet I'm not one to exaggerate. I believe that α-glycopeptides are the most important nutrient I've ever found. Soon you will understand that profound point. So I look forward to explaining this to you and we'll soon see if you agree.

I've been looking for a fundamental natural supplement for over 44 years—one that supports the entire body the way that the foundation and steel girders support a tall building. One that helps the body maintain all of its various life processes (metabolism, hormones, immunity, nerves, repair, detoxification, energy, etc.), and most importantly something that helps us feel terrific as we go about our daily lives.

I'm thrilled to tell you that we're blessed that such a marvelous food-compound now exists—thanks to a visionary entrepreneur—Russ Hall—who understands what ailing humanity needs to restore health. So he hired the world's leading rice geneticist to improve the source-food, secured the source materials, and invested millions of dollars in proprietary hydrolyzing/milling equipment to render healing molecules that the cells can instantly use. What's really great is that it's not expensive. And that's just the way it should be!

Now you can understand that this is personal—I truly mean what I'm saying—that this book is about the most important nutritional molecule with which you can supplement your diet to improve the quality of life for yourself, your family, and humanity. I intend to substantiate this point to you in these few pages, and then show you how you can prove it to yourself.

Like many people, I've used various super supplements that support the body in maintaining good health—things like organic greens-powders, organic plant minerals, organic whey protein drinks, mannose, ubiquinol[§], and various juice products such as noni, açaí, aloe, and mangosteen. The promises were great, the research compelling, and I continue to use various supplements everyday, but in clinical practice I get the best results form α-glycopeptides. As a clinician dedicated to genuinely healing programs, I gravitate toward consistent results.

In this book, we'll examine a product that, across the board, is helping the majority of people who take it. Not everyone raves about the benefits, but certainly many, even most, do. Rather than the touted good results being the exception (as with so many products on the market), with α-glycopeptides the rare exception is the person who does not experience a wonderful energy and wellbeing. Now that's a diametric turn around in statistics!

α-Glycopeptides[§]. Some researchers call them"the fountain of youth," some scientists designate them "the key to health and longevity," and I know two doctors who've labeled them the "miracle molecules." I call them *alpha glycopeptides* for short. Most people call them "polysaccharide/polypeptides," but henceforth in this book they are called *α-glycopeptides* to denote their tiny size (α-) and molecular configuration (glycopeptides.)

■ ENERGY IS EVERYTHING

Energy is the foundation of health. Energy and health are so closely allied in an healthy. If your body is healthy (properly nourished), it can make plenty of energy.

■ *Energy and persistence conquer all things.* – Ben Franklin

■ *Energy is eternal delight.* – William Blake

■ *Energy is the essence of life.* – Oprah Winfrey

Simply stated; α-glycopeptides are a tiny group of nutritional sugars attached to a tiny group of peptide proteins.

We all know that it's really not so important what other people *say* about something. That's their experience, their knowing. What's important is what we *know for ourselves*, so let's discover together exactly what these nutrients—this proprietary blend[2] of α-glycopeptides—are, and what they can do for your well-being. If you are in clinical practice, you will discover, what this nutrient can do for those trusting you to help them with their health.

It's All About Energy. *In human health, energy is everything.* Without cellular energy, we cannot have one clear thought, or the ability to digest our food, or the muscle power to walk, or the ability to sleep well. When our bodies have ample cellular energy, they can take care

---

2   The proprietary blend of α-glycopeptides of this discussion is manufactured exclusively by the Enzacta Corporation of Spring Park, MN in a proprietary process, and marketed under the trade name PXP® (for public distribution) as well as a separate physician's clinical formula. Only the Enzacta-produced products provide α-glycopeptides that are 99% absorbable. Yes, there are 'me, too' products, and more can be expected; but they do not compare to the Enzacta α-glycopeptide products as you'll soon see.

of all aspects of our health—general vitality, metabolic and hormonal processes, immune system effectiveness, nerve transmissions, all tissue functions, detoxification, and repair—with radiant effectiveness. Then, if something's amiss, that's what clinicians are for.

Further, when there is a lack of cellular energy, there are inevitable problems: the body ages more rapidly, tissues fail, hormones become less effective, arteries become hard, cellular communications get garbled, inflammations become chronic, fat gets stored, the brain becomes sluggish, the immune system becomes confused, and pathogens create problems. **With the human body, low cellular energy always leads to one disease or another. Always.**

Basically, when you run out of energy, you die. *Energy*, defined as the ability to do work, is absolutely and unequivocally required for every life process. And *work* is defined as a force that moves a mass, or causes potential energy to be converted into kinetic energy. But hey, we all know what work is in the practical sense. It takes energy.

> "I've been waiting for 30 years for this product! It's literally transforming the health of many people I know and I have many doctors trying it. I really think that this product could change the world. I've never seen anything like it."
>
> - Dr. Dan Clark, M.D., Florida

This book is the story about your body's ability to have its full compliment of energy. Energy precedes optimal health and optimal health requires energy. There's no way around it—energy is everything. Energy is Life. If you long for a taste of optimal health, you must have abundant cellular energy. No exceptions. Health is having vibrant energy.

Natural health practitioners, naturopaths, acupuncturists, osteopaths, homeopaths, complimentary medicine physicians, chiropractors, complimentary-practice dentists, clinical nutritionists, herbalists, massage and body work therapists, colon hygienists, and others, all wish to address the cause of a person's ailments and help the body heal itself. They analyze the patient, determine a probable cause of concern, and then implement the best strategy they know. Sometimes the symptoms[§] go away, sometimes they don't, depending upon whether or not the therapy accurately addressed the true cause, did not get stalled with obstacles, and was effective in stimulating the body to heal itself.

Helping people with their health can be complicated. Often there are multiple causes to a single symptom. One must aske the following questions: Is there a lifestyle issue? Is a pathogen such as a virus, bacteria, parasite, or fungus involved? Is the person hydrated? Are toxins blocking metabolic pathways? Is the person's pH (acid/alkaline balance) involved? Is an epigenetic[§] stimulus activating a disease gene expression? (The body requires energy, nutrients, and DNA repair to 'reset' or 'deactivate' an errant genetic expression.) Is chronic inflammation present? What about poor digestion, nutrient absorption, or constipation? Is the neuroendocrine (nerves/hormones) system confused? Are there high stress factors? You see, there are so many wheels-within-wheels with multi-dimensional human beings, and they all affect our equilibrium and health, e.g. the whole person.

> Inflammation is the process underlying both chronic degenerative diseases as well as autoimmune diseases. α-Glycopeptides help the body regulate its inflammation processes via its anti-inflammatory nutrients (antioxidants) as well as through the cell-signaling process. Most importantly, they provide cellular energy to allow the body to correct the underlying cause of inflammation.

> Health comes, of course, with the adjustment of the vibratory rates within one's self.
>
> P. Twitchell, *Herbs the Magic Healers*

> As I see it, every day you do one of two things: build health or produce disease in yourself.
>
> Adelle Davis

> God always takes the simplest way.
>
> Albert Einstein

If only there was one supplement that would address all these things and support the entire body with the energy it needs to heal itself. If only there was a supplement that would help practically everyone feel better and improve their health no matter what.

Throughout my natural health career, I've been guided by one cardinal question: What does it take for the body to be able to heal itself completely? I've never been interested in palliation, amelioration, control, coping, temporary relief, or suppressing symptoms. So my life work has been about genuine healing and maintaining optimal health. This quest has lead me to study vitamins, minerals, herbs, nutrients and remedies; to becoming a licensed clinical nutritionist, and then on to become a classical homeopath. It's taken me through modalities such as formal clinical nutrition education (biochemistry), functional laboratory testing, principles of acupuncture, herbal pharmacology, and numerous research studies. Always seeking 'The Answer' to what unlocks the puzzle box of each person's individual health concerns — how to facilitate healing within an individual.

If your body is tired, if you are expressing symptoms, if you are having pain, if your doctor has labeled you as having a disease, if your brain is foggy, if your weight is too high, if you need stimulants to get through the day, if you are concerned about aging, if your bones could be stronger, if your skin has blemishes and hair lacks luster — it means that your body is crying out for the one common denominator to all those circumstances. That one collective cry is for cellular energy. Why? Because with cellular energy, your body can correct its symptoms and restore its metabolic balance that speaks to you as a positive outlook, an ease about life, and general well being.

The body may also be crying out for water, phytonutrients, alkaline foods, enzymes, vitamins, minerals, and so forth; but none of those things work without cellular energy. Without cellular energy, the body cannot properly utilize nutrients and herbs. Even homeopathic remedies are dependent upon adequate cellular energy for the innate vital force§ to motivate the body to correct symptom-expressions. Cellular energy is the most profound 'energy adjustment' a person can facilitate nutritionally. **We live and die at the cellular level. Either we have Life energy or the cell dies.**

Alpha Glycopeptides. Since starting to work clinically with nutritional α-glycopeptides [proprietary glycoproteins§ comprised of a beneficial sugar molecule (glyco) attached to a beneficial protein molecule (peptide) that are small enough (alpha or α, smaller than one-billionth of a part) to be absorbed quickly into the cells, people report such wonderful improvements in their heath. What a joy it is to be the conduit for their newfound health, freedom, and life.

Here is a written testimonial excerpt from a lady who exemplifies what has become a wonderfully frequent occurrence. This comes from a two-page signed letter that includes her San Antonio, Texas phone number. I will not cite the nature of her health issue so this is not a claim of nutritional glycopeptides treating or helping any disease—which they did not do—because we all acknowledge that the α-glycopeptides simply provided her body with the nutritional energy it needed to heal itself.

I have had [name of condition] for 21 years. I had chronic fatigue, migraines, yeast infections (every week for 21 years), went blind in one eye a couple of times, I was very clumsy (breaking glasses, hitting chairs and could not walk properly), slept most of the day, and you get the idea. I could not perform my chores of things to do at home. I have always said, "When the mother of the house is ill, the entire household is ill." I had taken everything that the doctors told me to take. I did not see any improvements in my health. Medical expenses ran steep, and let me tell you that we were broke! My husband came home with a product that changed my life and my family's life forever. When he showed me the container, I almost laughed at him and told him that they "pulled your leg," that a nutritional product can't help me with a metabolic disorder. I have heard many things that people say (many on TV) of products that work, but really they do not work at all. But I saw that my husband was so excited, I just had to give it a chance, but the truth is that I felt that I was having the equivalent of chamomile tea or Rice Krispies®. I started to take the [glycopeptides] because he insisted and it did not taste bad at all. But I was sure it wouldn't help. But how wrong I was. I can tell you now, from the bottom of my heart, IT WORKS! My husband says that thanks to [glycopeptides], he's got his wife back. My life has completely changed for the better. The changes have been many. Back then, my normal day started at 11:00 a.m. and I had to go to bed at 6:30 p.m. because of my chronic fatigue. Now my normal day starts at 6:30 a.m. and I can go to 11:00 p.m. or 12 [midnight] with no trouble whatsoever. Now, I am active, happy and I feel really fantastic. Really, my life and the life of my family have changed (for the good) tremendously. It has changed so much that I and my husband feel that we have not only a moral obligation to share these benefits with the whole world, but we have an obligation to God to share our experience with everyone that listens to us. [Glycopeptides] are unique because they work! A recommendation: Be constant and have discipline taking the [glycopeptides], and keep taking it for 90-120 days. You will see the results (great benefits). God Bless You All. --T.S.

What's Health, Really? Health is much more than an absence of symptoms. It is a dynamic, adaptable balance between the body's self-regulatory processes (hormone directives, metabolic efficiency, energy production, nerve transmissions, detoxification, and repair processes) and the challenges of life—physically, emotionally, mentally, and spiritually. Health implies an "ease" in body performance coupled with an enthusiasm for living.

Here, we will present information about a simple, affordable, natural health breakthrough that may be exactly what you need to experience a more healthy vitality and provide your body with the cellular life-chemistry it needs to enjoy natural energy, stamina, immunity, clear thinking, and the creativity that is your birthright as a human being.

More healthy vitality means different things to different people, but for many it is a way to maintain a more biologically youthful body—one where maintaining proper weight is not based on struggle and restriction; where get-up-and-go is not centered around the jangle of caffeine; where bone density is not based on drugs that cause unwanted side effects; where alleviation of painful symptoms is not based on suppression; where

Health and happiness means to be rid of fatigue and disease. To have a good appetite, good memory, good humor, and precision in thought and action. To be free from anxiety and fear. To have a great capacity for survival over illness and anxieties. To have joy, long life, and great spiritual adventures.

P. Twitchell, *Herbs The Magic Healers*

graceful aging is not based on expensive, never-ending hormone augmentation; where a good night's sleep is not an accident; and where a satisfying love-life is not a rare occasion.

If all these good things are not based on struggles, drugs, and manipulations, then upon what exactly are they based? The answer is: the innate, normal functioning of your body, or simply put, having the energy for your body to work the way it's supposed to—the way it is designed to work. A more optimal state of health already exists inside your body. We are discussing a nutritional supplement that can help you realize this deep principle and excellent health.

The Blueprint of Health. Creationists say, "God designed the blueprint of our bodies to be perfect." Evolutionists say, "The body's blueprint is perfectly evolved and adapted to our niche in Nature." Either way, our bodies

Within your body is an innate intelligence — a regulatory mechanism that desires your optimal health. Thus the healer is within, and its proper performance requires energy.

have a perfect blueprint and an innate intelligence whose primary directive is to manifest that blueprint as best it can, adapt, and survive. Optimal health resides inside our cells, not in something that we pursue and acquire. It is something we facilitate from within. The facilitator is energy.

What about people who have inherited flaws in their bodies' ability to perform optimally? For example people with allergies or missing enzyme systems. The natural health model is most emphatically clear that there are healing modalities that help people overcome their inherited (genetic) flaws. I personally am one such case. The body can correct such flaws by resonating more compatibly with its optimal blueprint. This we know—whatever can be done to help people overcome symptoms of poor health, there must be adequate cellular energy to "fund the process."

Think for a minute – what you do if your bank account suddenly had millions of dollars in it? You could pay off your bills, buy a new home, car, boat, furniture, jet, or perhaps pay your taxes. You could improve your standard of living and life experience. You could support charities and help others. You could invest for the future. Money is the currency that operates the physical world. Cellular energy is the currency that operates your body. α-Glycopeptides fund your body's bank accounts to make you rich in health. Your body needs those funds to upgrade your health.

As a child, coming out from under the anesthesia and having my tonsils removed, I overhead two nurses having a conversation. One nurse said, "Why did God give us tonsils, and then we routinely remove them, even when they are not diseased? Why did God give us adenoids and appendixes, and for thousands of years we did not have the technology to remove those mistakes, but now we do? I don't see how those tissues can be mistakes. They must have a purpose." I recall having similar doubts, even at that early age, innately knowing that the body's blueprint is perfect and everything serves a purpose—

no extraneous parts. Nature is too exacting.

So why doesn't the body perform the way it should? I would soon learn that there is a simple cause-and-effect relationship with the Laws of Nature. The operative law underlying all life-processes is energy, and thus the law underlying and unifying the myriad disease processes is the lack of energy production in the cells. Paradoxically, even hyper-function diseases (overactive cellular expressions) can be associated with a lack of cellular energy because it takes energy to have the proper cell-signaling§ that would automatically reduce the hyper-functioning tissue or immune system. In the yin/yang of life, there are conditions of excessive energy (excessive heat, excessive inflammation). However those excesses are often in response to an element that is under functioning due to a lack of cellular energy such as inflammation of the cell membrane. The big picture issue today is the human energy crisis—just not enough cellular energy production to operate the body in optimal health.

Providing energy to the cells sounds simple enough until we try to "bell the cat." What must we do to have our bodies work the way they are intended to work? Our first and foundational point is this: it all starts with energy. Not with vitamins, minerals, enzymes, super nutrients, exotic juices, antioxidants, probiotics§, herbs, hormones, glandulars, or medicines.

Again, it all starts with energy, and energy production in the physical body is cellular, and it requires fuel including sugars and glycoproteins, nutrient molecules, water and oxygen. Therefore, our health is dependent upon getting the proper fuel into our cells. Once adquately fueled, our cells can perform their functions properly, and that means we can quickly experience a more optimal degree of health.

So simply put, this book is about how to properly fuel your cells so that they can do everything their innate blueprint endows, and that endowment is optimal health. It should come as no surprise that this cellular endowment includes increased physical energy, normalization of weight, stronger bones, healthy performance of immune system activities, maintenance of youthfulness, effective expression of libido, increased creativity, retraction of symptoms, and a healthy resistance to chronic degenerative diseases.

A helpless baby cries when he or she needs help. That cry is the universal language for assistance. Our bodies are like babies. They cry out with symptoms to let us know we need to render assistance. Symptoms should not be suppressed, but understood and the cause corrected. The fundamental and universal requirement for the body to correct symptoms is cellular energy (called ATP) that is made by the mitochondria organelle inside the cells. With a shortage of ATP, the body cannot correct its symptoms.

Your body was not designed to be sick, in pain, or have chronic-degenerative diseases. If you have symptoms, your body is crying out for help. It needs more energy at the cellular level so it can figure out and implement necessary adjustments to its life processes.

Within every cell in your body resides the directive, knowledge, and expertise for you to live a life of vitality and to have the optimal health you deserve. Energy unleashes the expression of that innate directive.

Why do you deserve it? Because optimal health is encoded in your genes. It's innate, foundational, and fundamental. Even for people born with genetic anomalies, epigenetic§ activations of unwanted responses, and handicaps, your body has an innate, primal drive to optimize health as best it can. We often have no idea how good it can get unless we boost our cellular energy so our bodies can perform more optimally.

Oftentimes, small things matter. Here is an early report from a lady in Kerrville, Texas (and there would be more positive reports to come over time.)

"I haven't had a good night's sleep in over 20 years. Thanks to
[α-glycopeptides] I've now discovered what a good night's sleep is." – L.P.

So what does this mean for you? Maybe it's about putting the spring back in your step, or dispelling the fog from your brain. Perhaps it's about unleashing the creativity that you know is inside of you. For many people it's about helping the body re-regulate the myriad warning signs of metabolic confusions (symptoms of less than optimal performance) and aging. Meaning it's all about having our bodies get rid of the cause of aches, pains, and symptoms of less than optimal health. Ground zero for beneficial changes is cellular energy which can turn the energy lights up a little brighter.

α-Glycopeptides – Miracle Molecules. For many of us, supplementing our diets with the 'miracle molecules' (α-glycopeptides) means that our bodies can now perform their metabolic functions better. A big part of this better performance means that our bodies correct a wide array of less than optimal performances all by themselves— if, and only if, they have the cellular energy to do so. We all instinctively realize that no one knows better than our bodies how to maintain and restore healthy life-processes, and here in these pages, you'll soon learn how to help your body harness it's innate resources to restore and maintain the best of health.

> Thanks a lot, much appreciated. Usually when I try to remember something I can't even go there, but this last week I thought, "Where did I see that advertisement? Immediately I remembered where. I haven't done that in a very long time. I'm getting things done I've needed to do for a long time and that feels good.
>
> Laura

In this book, you'll find out why some people are using superlatives to describe their results after taking "the miracle molecules" consistently for even a short time. In looking over the testimonials of people describing their newly found health, we find that superlatives such as: "Phenomenal!", "Wow!", "Fountain of Youth!", "Thank God", "Wonderful!", "Fantastic!", "Energized!", "God-Send", "Fabulous", "New Life!" and "Marvelous!" abound in people's personal experiences after supplementing their diets with the simple, organic, whole-food-derived molecule known as α-glycopeptides. Also please understand that not everyone has a superlative experience in just a short time, some people need a little longer, some need to support other facets of their health such as improved nutritional intake, but it all starts with cellular energy and perseverance certainly pays off.

Over the past several years, α-glycopeptides have been available and enthusiastically received as a natural health-food supplement in Mexico, and they've also been available for some time in the Philippines, Spain, Guatemala, El Salvador, Ecuador, Columbia, and Korea. From those countries there are thousands of reports of health improvements that often labeled as "miraculous." There are hundreds of medical physicians that have direct experience of seeing the body's innate healing abilities once the cells are provided with energy derived from α-glycopeptides. Now it's available in the United States with other countries soon to come.

At the time of this writing, α-glycopeptides, in a completely assimilable form, have been available in the United States as an over-the-counter natural health supplement for only a short time. In the USA, as in the other countries, medical doctors are often the major proponents. However being a natural health product, everyone has direct access to trying α-glycopeptides for themselves to ascertain its benefits by personal experience.

As would be expected, α-glycopeptides are now experiencing an escalation of devotees in the United States with first-hand experience of its health enhancing properties. But is it right for you? Will you join those who have experienced dramatic improvements in neurological communications, blood sugar regulation, muscle and bone strength, digestion and elimination, creativity, nervous system functions, immunological processes, energy, and overall wellbeing? Let's find out.

Factual Honesty. You may have heard of or tried "revolutionary health breakthroughs" before that seem to help others, but never seem to help you. As a licensed, natural health clinician, I certainly have. This is often the case with unscrupulous marketers who take the one-in-twenty-thousand testimonial and present it like it happens that way for everyone. I'm thankful to say that this is not the case with the α-glycopeptides we are discussing. First, I commit to you that I will never do that. Second, thousands of testimonials abound, and part of this book's mission is to teach you how to use α-glycopeptides so that they work for you as well. Personal experience is the truth you seek. It's that simple!

It is my experience that if your life experience is being undermined by a lack of cellular energy, then most assuredly α-glycopeptides will improve your life experience in dramatic ways. For many people, this means that fatigue and confusion and hundreds of annoying symptoms can evaporate like puddles in the hot sun.

According to Dr. Luis Romero, a Harvard and University of Massachusetts-trained medical doctor, one of the world's leading experts, and passionate proponent of, α-glycopeptides, "You absolutely and unequivocally must feed your cells every day. This is the only way to maintain optimal health. And the best way to do that is to supplement your life with alpha-glycopeptides."

My α-glycopeptides story. I would not be writing this book for you if I did not personally experience benefits from taking α-glycopeptides. Being a bit of a health nut, I don't have many body complaints. My personal experience is this: I took one scoop a day for three weeks. Did not notice much. So I took 3 scoops a day and just two days later had a noticeable improvement in calm-energy, mental creativity and better sleep. Something definitely shifted and there was a new ease in living. Since that day of recognizing improvements, I have continued to use α-glycopeptides and have experienced cumulative benefits of much better sustained energy. Life just seems brighter, I feel joy and contentment (despite the rigors of life) more frequently, and I have greater enthusiasm for life. We could say that this book is fueled by α-glycopeptides because writing this book is just one outlet for this newfound energy. At 60 years old, I feel like I'm 30. (I felt like 40 prior to α-glycopeptides.) And that's a terrific thing. Based on, "it works for me," I have now recommended α-glycopeptides to more than 200 people who also affirm an amazingly wide array of benefits that I will share with you in these pages.

You will soon read about naturally-derived α-glycopeptides—where they come from, how they're processed, and what your body can do with them. But most importantly, this information will help you discover for yourself how you could be a beneficiary of improved cellular energy via α-glycopeptides by taking the questionnaires included here. This book should inspire you to take the α-Glycopeptide Challenge to gain irrefutable, personal proof that it is important to your health, well-being, and quality of life.

What is the α-Glycopeptide Challenge? Simply this: start by taking α-glycopeptides every day for a month. If you like what you experience, then raise the amount for another month to get a stronger picture, and reevaluate. There's nothing like personal experience to prove the efficacy of all this information, and it's a short and exciting 60 days when you start noticing cumulative improvements. So you will soon learn that proponents of α-glycopeptides put their money where their cells' mouths are, and that's exactly where α-glycopeptides belong— helping your cells function better, so your tissues function better, so your body functions better, so your life functions better.

Good, healthy living is what we all want! So here we find that supplementing with α-glycopeptides improves the quality of life. For young and old, having a full compliment of cellular energy means a life without limiting symptoms, fatigue, and distracting pains. True to our definition of optimal health, it means a life of vitality, energy, and dynamic wellbeing.

Natural health practitioners usually take or have taken the very supplements that they recommend. Thus the natural health practitioners have first-hand experience with the supplements they use and know how they taste, how they feel in the tummy, how they help the body, and if they cause any side-show symptoms such as cleansing reactions. Here is a program for natural health practitioners and physicians interested in helping their patients nutritionally, who first use the supplements themselves for personal experience.

Dr. Dan Clark says, "Based on all the research I've studied regarding polysaccharide-peptides [α-glycopeptides], it would not surprise me if taking α-glycopeptides regularly would add ten to fifteen years of good, healthy living to a person's lifespan."

■ GLYCOPEPTIDE CHALLENGE

- **Days 1-30: Upon Arising (Empty Stomach)**

  Mix 1 heaping Tsp. α-Glycopeptides in room temperature or warm water. Stir and drink immediately.

  Note: very sensitive people should consider starting with 1 skimpy Tsp., then increase.

  That's all there is to it. Do that for 30 days and evaluate. With some noticeable improvements, you should be encouraged to test it a bit further, so let's increase the amount and really get acquainted with the benefits of α-glycopeptides.

- **Days 31-60: Upon Arising (Empty Stomach)**

  Mix 2 level Tsp. α-Glycopeptides in room temperature or warm water. Drink immediately.

  Late Afternoon (Before Supper, Empty Stomach)

  Mix 2 level Tsp. α-Glycopeptides in room temperature water. Drink immediately.

Panacea? Since we are focusing on something exciting that inevitably helps everyone in some way, let me state that as a clinician, researcher, and seeker of true healing practices, "There is no such thing as a panacea that you pick up and take." That means that there is not a product or medicine or food or substance that can cure everyone of all of their ailments. It just doesn't exist and in fact, it **can't exist**.

Each human being has a personal life experience and there is no physical "instant cure," available across the board, particularly when we understand fully that what manifests in our lives is based on cause-and-effect principles stemming from what we believe, think, and feel, as well as from what we do and don't do. We are each biochemically individual.

With most people, a primary cause of their health concerns is simply the lack of cellular energy and effective cellular communications. Having cellular energy is a prerequisite to enabling the body to self-correct. Cells respond to

> There is no such thing as an on-demand panacea for human health. But glycopeptides come as close to one as I've ever seen!

α-glycopeptides immediately and provide the numerous exciting testimonials that I'm hearing now almost every day at my consulting desk.

Other people have concerns that not only require more cellular energy, but also require their bodies to correct an aberrant metabolic behavior. They need energy and cellular communication molecules for their bodies to figure something out (share messages throughout the body), detoxify, remove pathogens, repair weak tissues, and adjust to better hormone receptivity. These are the people who are reporting cumulative benefits over a longer time as in four to six months.

> **The Universal Panacea**
> Love cures people, the ones who receive love and the ones who give it, too.
>
> Karl Menninger

There are also people who are very low on the energy-survival scale. They have worn out tissues, weak collagen, high toxicity, acidic pH, depression, obesity, poor cell-signaling, weariness, and need a complete overhaul of their health. Their bodies must go through an extensive rebuilding and reorganization process. Daily use of α-glycopeptides is the turning point. Consistent use over a year's time provides improved cellular energy and cell-signaling communications so the body can reclaim its most optimal health according to its innate abilities.

The One and Only Genuine Panacea. There is only one panacea in Life, and it's called "Love," meaning an attitude of good will, often expressed by a detached caring for others based on respect of their right to experience Life on their own terms. Love is the only universal cure. It is the only vibrational force that can universally correct aberrations of the mind and heart, provided a person can accept it. More than any other single health product I've ever encountered, α-glycopeptides are helping sio many people experience improved health.

Further, a person's less-than-optimal health expressions might be predicated on more than one dysfunction. Of course there is a lack of cellular energy and replenishing that energy is absolutely necessary for there to be genuine and lasting improvement. There could also be mechanical dysfunctions from injuries, loss of innate intestinal flora, overly acidic pH, subclinical infections (root canal, abscess, chronic appendix inflammation, cavitation). These must be addressed along the road toward more optimal health.

Summary Statement. As a clinician, I also know that all healing comes from within. I also know that healing is simply an adjustment of a person's vibratory rate, and thus all healing is an "energy adjustment." I personally love the energy adjustment that occurs when people provide their cells with the fuel and communication molecules that they need to serve their larger range of expression called "Life."

Before we delve into our discussion on how your cells make energy, here is a testimonial that made this week extra special for me.

7/2010, I would like to share my [α-glycopeptide] experience with you and whomever you would like to pass this along to.

I am a firm believer in natural/holistic practices as I would not have my daughter today if I had relied on conventional medicine. When you contacted me in reference to glycopeptides I was more than ready to give it a try. I was hoping for help in the following areas: I was feeling sluggish, foggy headed, forgetful, tired, and I needed some energy. Little did I realize that I could have help with a situation I had never discussed with you because I didn't think it was something that could be helped.

I will be 38 in two months and have had lower back and hip pain since my early 20's. I have one leg that is shorter than the other and in my early 20's spent a great deal of time and money in the chiropractor's office with this problem. When it would get unbearable I would go for massages and adjustments with my chiropractor (I have a very high tolerance for pain). As I got older picking up my children hurt, getting down on the ground to sit Indian-style made it almost impossible to get up and walk, It hurt to get down to bathe my daughter (I did it in the sink for as long as I could, got her to stand on a chair and I helped her in), lifting them to get into the car seat was painful but the most impossible was moping/vacuuming and going to the grocery store and pushing a basket loaded with groceries. For the last four years I would take my husband with me to push the basket or I couldn't stand the pain that followed. I would take 3-4 Advil® several times a day and it didn't take away the pain. My husband would tease me "we can rebuild you!" I thought I needed a hip replacement or maybe had bad arthritis and that the pain was related to my leg situation. My MD would give me pain-killers and muscle relaxers that I wouldn't take because I didn't like how they made me feel. The last year it has become so bad to where I couldn't even sleep on my left hip because it hurt so bad. I would lay in bed unable to sleep because of the pain and just cry. We even purchased a $3200 Tempurpedic® mattress thinking that would help but it didn't.

After two days on the [α-glycopeptides] (just one scoop a day is what I started on) I noticed that I was not in any pain! I was on my feet all day long and I should have been in misery at that time but I wasn't. I thought let me think about this.....could it be the [α-glycopeptides]? That is exactly what it was. I get in bed at night and I'm so excited because I am not in pain. I went to the grocery store yesterday all by myself and after $160 worth of groceries loaded down in my basket...no pain. I have a housekeeper that comes specifically for my floors because we recently purchased a home and there is no carpet so the entire 2400 sq ft home needs to be mopped and vacuumed. I helped with that today and I am not in pain. As of now I can't say if α-glycopeptides have helped me with *what I originally started taking it for because I am so overjoyed that I am not in pain I can't think of anything else!!*

I am increasing my α-glycopeptides intake to 2-3 times per day to see where that will take me. I thank God for this product and you because I can enjoy my life and family pain free.

- God's Blessings, A. M. A., Ganado, TX

So let's start at the very beginning and learn a bit about this healthimproving, life enhancing nutritional molecule — α-glycopeptides. To set that stage, let's first review how our cells make the "energy of life."

Cellular Energy – The Dividing Line Between Health and Disease

Here is a brief and simple discussion on how our cells make energy. By understanding this summary, you will understand a primary key to better health and longevity. To explain this, we'll delve into some biochemistry and use some scientific terms, (I'll do my best to make it simple) and at the end of any molecule discussions, I'll summarize the important points in a summary box. The molecule discussion serves as the background and the summary points that follow present the reason for the discussion. Here we go.

One of the reasons that human beings have survived over time, and become the current dominant species on Earth, is that our bodies have multiple ways to produce the energy we need to survive. Fundamentally, we human beings derive energy from the sun through the photosynthesis of plants. The plants make nutritional molecules (sugars, fats, and proteins) and we eat the plants and provide our bodies with that converted form of solar energy—vital sugars of which *glucose* is the most notorious and well known, but there are other healing sugars that are indispensable to our life processes as well. Please know that even more important than healing sugars are the protein facets of the α-glyco*peptides*. A glycopeptide is a happy marriage between healing sugars and healing proteins known as *peptides*. (We'll discuss the peptide molecule in just a bit.) In the case of meat eaters (human and predatory animals), the prey-animal eats the plant and derives the solar energy that is then passed along to the carnivore. Inevitably, *life begets life*.

Life begets life is one of the critically important "Laws of Life" and it means that our foods as human beings must come from living things— in the current state of human nutrition this refers to both plants and animals as that is the currently accepted standard on planet Earth. The more that we introduce "dead" and "changed" foods (chemicals, preservatives, trans fats, irradiated, overcooked, genetically-modified, microwaved, processed) to our diets, the more the body becomes estranged from its foundational health systems and the inevitable result is disease. We all know that our bodies respond to fresh picked foods—our genes teach us that fresh foods taste better and they impart more life-energy. You know our credo: *Energy is Everything!*

This means that human beings depend upon plants for food energy, as well as for their role in the oxygen/carbon dioxide cycle of life. Vegetation and simple life forms that photosynthesize sunlight— *cyanobacteria* and *plankton* in the ocean—produce oxygen that our cells need to make energy. Because of plants, we have both the food and oxygen we need to produce energy. Human life is unequivocally based on a very intimate relationship with plants and plant like lifeforms.

> **IT'S ALL ABOUT CELLULAR ENERGY**
>
> A lack of cellular energy is synonymous with cellular aging, so we are only as young as our cellular energy and the mitochondria that produce it.

As previously mentioned, energy is synonymous with Life Itself. So from an overview perspective, let's take a simple journey through the body's energy process, because in doing so, we'll discover the reason that α-glycopeptides are helping so many people improve their health.

Energy Starts With Food-Nutrition. We all know that our bodies require food for energy. This is why we get hungry. Our bodies warn us that our ready-fuel is running low.

We also know that our digestive processes are responsible for breaking down food molecules into the three **macro-nutrient** food categories— proteins, fats, and carbohydrates—which are then absorbed through our stomachs and intestines where they move through the blood and lymph to the liver where they are "humanized[§]" if necessary and rendered to be "self" and not foreign. However, if small enough, some molecules are immediately grabbed by the cells because they are recognized as being ready to go to work. Further, food can provide other factors for good health—probiotics, soil-based organisms, alkaline mineral reserves, nascent water, micro-nutrients (vitamins and minerals), and insoluble fiber.

We also absorb other nutritional health factors from our food, the **micro-nutrients**: vitamins, minerals, enzymes, coenzymes, humates (humic and fulvic acid), and other nutritive factors such as antioxidants. Micro-nutrients are generally not used for fuel so they are not burned for energy. They serve the body's metabolism in other life-supporting processes including the rendering of energy from food and tissue support.

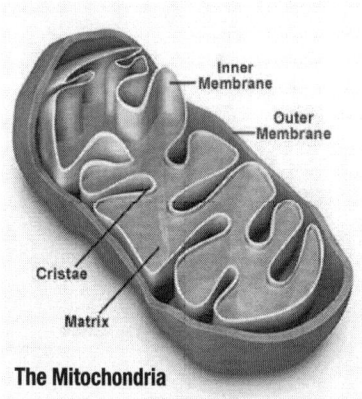

Inner Membrane

Outer Membrane

Cristae

Matrix

The Mitochondria

Macro-nutrients are used in making fuel as well as tissue structures such as cell membranes, nerve sheaths, bones and muscles. This means that the human body requires proteins and fats, as well as the well-known carbohydrates (glucose and healing sugars), to provide fuel.

While the simple sugar, glucose, is most touted for energy, the most optimal fuel source for all the activities of the body includes availability of all three macro-nutrients—protein, carbohydrate, and fat, although the carbohydrate, glucose, is the predominant fuel. People who eat too much processed sugar (table sugar, high fructose sweetener) do indeed get lots of the wrong kind of energy with the result that they become obese (energy stored as fat), and suffer from high blood pressure, high cholesterol, and diabetes. Glucose is an excellent fuel for energy when the body manufacturers it for the cells from complex carbohydrates. However, it's not so beneficial when industry processes it from cane and beets, and then people eat refined sugar (dextrose, fructose, high fructose corn and agave sweeteners.) The human body is made to operate on a complex fuel blend. Our cellular engines require a diesel-type fuel (glycopeptides, glycolipids[§]), not just rocket fuel (glucose).

Now to understand energy at the cellular level, we need to know that inside the cells are specific power generating organelles called *mitochondria*[§]. These energy generators are necessary for the life of practically every kind of cell in our bodies (red blood cells excepted), and each cell can contain over 2500 mitochondria. With one nucleus and 2500 mitochondria, we could say that our cells are obsessed with energy, and rightly so, because in Life, "Energy is everything!" (And I bet you've heard that before!)

As the human body ages, the number of functional mitochondria decreases and elderly people often have less energy than younger people. The decline in the number of mitochondria may not be a function of time, but instead it's a function of the lack of energy needed to protect and repair all cellular processes including the maintenance of mitochondria.

> Mitochondria are our fountains of youth, and we have millions and millions of them. And the healing elixir they pour forth is called ATP[§] (Adenosine TriPhosphate, the body's life energy.)

When the mitochondria have a short supply of oxygen and fuel to make ATP properly, they can have their specific genetics damaged by the very free radicals (rogue electrons) that result from making energy. This is the start of the life destroying mitochondrial diseases that we'll soon discuss.

Also, as cells lose their identity (*telomeres*[§] on the ends of DNA strands) due to free radical damage in the cell nucleus, the cells lose their ability to function properly. Why did they lose their identity? Lack of energy.

Since the mitochondria have their own genetic code and require energy to repair and maintain themselves, they suffer when environmental and metabolic toxins choke off their oxygen and nutrient supply. When additional energy is available, the cells repair their DNA via enzymes and glycopeptides. This is why cellular energy is so important—it keeps our bodies young.

Natural Free Radical Protection. The mitochondria create free radical[§] electrons as a by-product of producing ATP. The mitochondria also produce the antioxidants to immediately capture and neutralize the free radicals, and even use the resulting molecules to derive more energy. So all should be in order according to Nature's plan. But unfortunately, human beings are suffering from an alarming increase in the amount of free radical damage and this is why antioxidant supplements are highly touted and such big sellers in the health food industry.

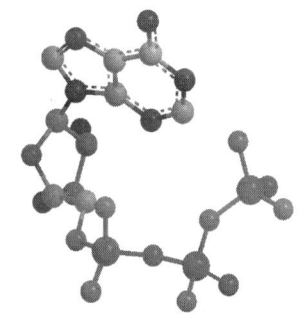

One theory of mitochondrial decline is that without adequate energy, the mitochondria are unable to control the free radicals and thus become damaged by their own metabolic by-products. Today's diet is simply not including enough fruit and vegetables to keep the mitochondria supplied with the raw materials (phytonutrients such as anthocyanins[§]) to function properly and thus we have the fact that our errant diets are the primary cause of all of our diseases.

Anthocyanins and Proanthocyanins. Fruit, vegetables, and special super strains of rice (purple rice) provide a special class of nutrient bioflavanoid complexes called anthocyanins and proanthocyanins. These are the molecules that give fruit, berries and seeds their red, blue, and purple colors such as the purple color of the special strain of rice used to render α-glycopeptides. The α-glycopeptides are rich in these valuable nutrients.

Research on anthocyanins and proanthocyanins shows them to help prevent tumors, reduce inflammations, repair collagen and injured tissues, reduce allergic reactions, prevent blood vessel damage, protect and sharpen the vision, prevent peroxynitrite (free radical) damage to the brain, protect against diabetic retinopathy, and many other critically important functions. So the naturally occurring anthocyanins and proanthocyanins are a tremendous asset to the nutritional support of α-glycopeptides because of their profound and comprehensive benefits.

Cut To The Chase – Summary #1

Test yourself and see if you understand these few points.

Cellular energy is a dividing line between: 1) health VS disease, 2) regeneration of tissue vs rapid aging, 3) optimal VS sub-optimal health.

- Human nutrition is founded on the Sun's energy rendered through plants.
- Nutrition must be accepted into the cells.
- The cells only accept "alpha" size (very tiny) molecules through the cell wall.
- α-Glycopeptides are alpha sized molecules that provide "glyco" molecules for energy and "peptides" for repair of tissue and DNA.
- Mitochondria (tiny organelles inside cells) produce the body's energy—ATP
- ATP is the body's chemical energy of life.
- ATP is essential for health, maintenance, repair, and function.
- Without adequate ATP energy, the cells and body cannot perform all it's health promoting, self-regenerative functions, and thus deteriorations occur.
- Mitochondria produce damaging, rogue electrons called free radicals as a by-product of making ATP energy, but they immediately neutralize free radicals with antioxidants.
- If nutrition is inadequate, there is a lack of antioxidants to manage free radicals.
- Free radicals damage the mitochondria and cause low cellular energy.
- Low cellular energy allows free radicals to damage DNA (the cell's life code).
- Damaged DNA results in mitochondrial diseases and aberrant cell behaviors.
- Proper nutrition helps the body generate energy and prevent free radical damage.
- We live and die at the cellular level.

α-Glycopeptide supplementation targets the cells – it provides the fuel for ATP energy as well as anti-oxidants to help quench free radicals.

Athletes Love α-Glycopeptides. One interesting fact about mitochondria is that most cells can create more of these energy generators if the body perceives it needs more energy and has the fuel and oxygen available to do so. Thus athletes' muscles generate more mitochondria as their muscles make demands for more energy from their aerobic and anaerobic exercises.

> "I just completed the most intensive, week-long workout with a new boot-camp training program and must admit that I've impressed myself with my level of stamina and lack of muscle soreness.
> I should have been very sore after that extreme exertion and it just didn't happen. You were right when you said that increased cellular energy could help process the lactic acid and turn it into energy. I love this stuff."
>
> Professional Athlete

When there is a full supply of mitochondrial fuel for energy production, the cells are able to recycle lactic acid — the metabolic waste product from exercise — and turn it into more ATP. Lactic acid is what makes the muscles sore after exercise. But with adequate ATP production, the cells can use lactic acid and thus the muscles don't get sore.

In my work, I'm privileged to work with numerous world-class, elite athletes—many at the top of their professions. The one universal statement from these professional athletes is this, "Glycopeptides help my muscles recover faster. I don't have soreness after a particularly strenuous competition."

What can you do with optimal energy? Think about this. If you don't have enough fuel for your body, the mitochondria shut down or go dormant. There's just not enough work to do. If you have a good dietary intake of macro-nutrients that are properly assimilated, then the mitochondria are all happy in their work because there is plenty of fuel. If you have abundant macro-nutrient intake and exercise that increase oxygen, the cells respond to that lifestyle and make more mitochondria (mitochondrial biogenesis), that in turn, make more energy for you. Thus the equation: **More energy = More life**.

One of the reasons that 'couch potatoes' (people who are lethargic and don't get exercise) don't feel so good, become obese, and get heart disease, is that their bodies don't get enough oxygen (aerobic metabolism) to make the energy that their bodies require for all the basic life processes.

With extra energy, your body can perform the functions of optimal health – repair tissue, protect cells that are reproducing, fight foreign invaders, destroy aberrant cells, make a vibrant personality, repair and protect the cells' DNA (genetic code), burn up toxins and detoxify cellular wastes efficiently, have radiant skin and hair, and have all your tissues work properly. Tissues that work properly do not allow diseases to occur. This is why we say that the very best of health is already inside your body. Your body just needs energy to release your innate optimal health blueprint. Now back to our dietary energy story.

As the dietary nutrients are made available to a cell for energy, the cell must engage in a complex process to render energy with the least amount of work. Nature adheres to a directive called the "Law of Economy" to make the most energy with the least amount of energy expenditure. This process involves the help of micro-nutrients such as vitamins, minerals and enzymes.

Dietary Law of Energy: What you eat must impart more energy to your body than it takes to digest, assimilate, transport nutrients through the cell walls and eliminate the waste products.

Dietarily, to be on the positive side of the energy equation, a person must derive more energy from food than it takes to digest, process, and transport it through the cell wall into the cell, and detoxify the wastes. This is the fundamental and immutable case for having a diet that is significant in certain raw foods.

Raw foods contain the enzymes that help the body digest and assimilate their nascent nutrients. Their molecules are intact the way that Nature made them as opposed to being altered by heat or processings, or even worse, genetically-modified.

When people consult with me to improve their diets, I counsel that the first thing to do is to take α-glycopeptides to prime the pump of cellular energy to prepare the body to best utilize the return to a natural diet. The proprietary α-glycopeptides we are discussing do not require a strong digestion to assimilate—they are ready for cellular absorption.

The Law of Economy is predominant throughout Nature. All Life seeks to function as best it can with the least amount of energy expenditure. This law permeates the natural actions of life. Trees will reach for the sun knowing that their energy expenditure will be rewarded when their leaves break through the top of the canopy. A cactus is an efficient water holding structure. Pollens release on a windy day. Throughout Nature is an innate intelligence that knows how to utilize energy—only Humankind has committed the ignorant and indulgent crime of waste and overuse of energy resources. Nature conserves energy, and the species that handle energy the best are the ones that survive.

Right here, at the cell's front door is where many people are struggling with their health. If the foods they are eating are damaged (overcooked, combined with chemical food additives such as Aspartame®, mono-sodium glutamate, and unnatural chemical preservatives). If they include trans-fats such as partially-hydrogenated oils, or they lack their innate nutrients as do processed foods grown on mineral-depleted soil with chemical fertilizers contain xenobiotic§ substances (pesticides, herbicides, fungicides, chemicals), have their molecular structures altered (Genetically-Modified foods), or certain nutrients are deficient due to dietary indiscretions (poor food choices, excessive alcohol), or digestion is impaired due to stress and dietary abuse, then it's the cells that suffer. *We live and die at the cellular level.*

As you can tell, practically everyone's cells are suffering due to dietary issues. The two body systems that are most susceptible to environmental toxins are: enzyme systems and, hormonal systems, and this is where we are finding so many of the health concerns occurring today. Perhaps this is one reason that people respond so favorably to supplementation with α-glycopeptides—after a long cellular famine, abundant fuel is instantly provided and the cells say, "Finally! Let's get to work! Let's reclaim health! Let's be all we can be!"

The cellular "front door" refers to the cell membrane, a selectively permeable screen through which the food nutrients must pass. The only nutrients that can pass through the cell membrane are "alpha" sized molecules which are very, very small—less than one billionth of a unit (10^{-9}) or between 1 and 100 nanometers. The purpose of digestion and the enzymes that split molecules and render the food to the 'alpha' size is simply this—they reduce the large food molecules to a size the cells can use. Dr. Luis Romero refers to α-glycopeptides as being "nano-nized" and thus are "bio-ready" for the body to use with a minimal amount of energy expenditure.

With the cell, size matters, and the smaller the better. This means that large molecules are barred at the door, but nucleo-proteins (one, two, and three chain peptides), tiny molecules of essential fats, and only simple sugars (such as glucose, galactose, ribose, n-acetyl-glucosamine, fucose), can pass the gatekeepers of the cell membrane.

The Energy "Catch 22§". As a side note, the cell wall is a separate organ with innate intelligence of its own. Many people's cell membranes are damaged from the effects of oxidative stress, and this is why so many people take antioxidant nutrients to counter the damaging effects of air pollution and trans-fats in the diet. However, the very best antioxidants are those that are produced by the cells themselves. And what do you think the cells need, in addition to nutritious food, to produce just the right antioxidants? Yes, it's energy. It's ATP.

When more energy is produced inside the cell by the mitochondria, the cell can synthesize its own antioxidants and use fatty acids in the diet to repair the cell membrane. So energy is the key. The "Catch 22" is that the mitochondria needs the fuel to help repair and maintain the cell membrane, but the fuel, as well as hormone-messages and oxygen can't pass through the cell membrane in the proper quantity. This is because the cell membrane is damaged by environmental pollution (pesticides and industrial toxins), free radical damage, dehydration, dietary indiscretions (poor food choices), and a lack of the energy necessary to maintain the cell membrane.

If only we could prime the pump or jump-start the repair process by getting a perfect fuel through the cell membrane to the mitochondria. And that's exactly what nutritional α-glycopeptides help the body do! Why? Because they're just the right size and molecular structure (thanks to the proprietary milling process and hydrolyzation) to pass through the cell's membranes and jump-start the healing energy processes. Further, the α-glycopeptide molecules provide a free proton, and thus contribute to the "proton pump[§]" process of nutrient induction into the cells. Ready-to-go α-glycopeptides can help the body resolve the paradoxical situation of the cell's energy crisis.

This also accounts for why some people notice the effects of α-glycopeptides immediately, but others require a little time for the pump-priming process to gain momentum from a cumulative process of daily use over time. Clinicians often encourage people to use α-glycopeptides per the tenets of the "α-glycopeptide challenge" where the cumulative effects are noticed over 60 days. Many people notice benefits in the first few days to two weeks, most by two months, and a few need a little longer for various individual reasons.

Of course, there are the rare few that may not notice anything- possibly because they run all day on caffeine, or simply are not in tune with their bodies, or their body's innate intelligence dictates that the initial increase of fuel be allocated to behind the scenes work, or had plenty of cellular energy so the additional fuel was inconsequential. Drs. Clark and Romero both mentioned to me that their patients who do not report self-noticed improvements still have dramatic improvements that are captured via laboratory blood tests. From my personal experience, I can tell you that most people cite noticeable benefits and love what I call that "ATP Feeling" of balanced energy and wellbeing called "Inner Strength".

A Tiny Bit of Your Body's Energy Cycle Simplified! The conversion of macro-nutrients into energy occurs in the cells and there is a specific process for each of the macro-nutrients to be converted to a substance known as *acetyl coenzyme A* (Acetyl-CoA). It's helpful to understand that proteins, fats, and carbohydrates can be converted to the "energy starter molecule" *Acetyl-CoA* if they are to be used for energy production.

This is a survival feature for human beings. If the only food you can acquire is fat, then the body will perform "beta-oxidation" and turn that fat into the raw material of energy—*Acetyl-CoA*. If the only food between you and starvation is protein, then the cells can render it into *Acetyl-CoA* via a process known as "deamination." And if you only have carbohydrates for survival, the body can hydrolyze the starch molecules and convert the chief carbohydrate, glucose, to *Acetyl-CoA* via a process known as "glycolysis."

The point in telling you this is that our food nutrients have specific pathways to get on the energy conveyer belt. It confirms our prior point about how these three energy-deriving systems assist the innate vitality's directive to adapt and survive. Once food nutrients are converted to the uniform molecule, *Acetyl-CoA*, they are ready for the mitochondria to work its miracle of creating life-energy.

Understanding that the body has a '"fuel conveyer belt" that addresses proteins, carbohydrates and fats, we find the basis for the health-destroying impact that table sugar has on our health. Table sugar crashes into the conveyer belt like a raging bull in a china shop. It hurdles through the body's meticulously planned processes and collides with the mitochondria, forcing energy production into the red zone. It's the same as if you put jet fuel in your car's gas tank. Refined sugar damages the cells and mitochondria, and leads to mitochondrial diseases.

The processes to turn food into the raw material of energy has a different level of efficiency. Each process has its own nutritional requirements and each process serves a different purpose such as the quick, but not lasting, energy of glycolosis that is needed for the "flight or fight" survival response as opposed to the slow and steady fuel supply associated with well-being that is made by the mitochondria. Glycolosis, is an anaerobic process that does not utilize oxygen to make instant energy. It is inefficient as it only renders two molecules of energy per molecule of carbohydrate, but because it can produce energy so quickly, it's a short-term way to respond to emergency situations.

This means that if a really hungry saber tooth tiger jumped out of the bushes and surprised you, your body would have instant energy to flee—all because of glycolosis' ability to throw some instant fuel on your muscle cells' fires. But your fleeing won't last long, and if you have to run far, your body will have to use the normal glucose-to-energy processes of the mitochondria; and if you have to run really, really far, your body will use the fat-conversion processes. Thus glycolosis works fine for a short sprint, the mitochondrial energy processes (Krebs Cycle) are terrific for a nice jog around the park, and the fat burning process, beta-oxidation, is particularly useful for a marathon. All energy systems work together to provide the human being with a wide range of responses and life activities as well as a strong survival position in Nature.

So you see, our bodies have multiple ways to derive energy for a variety of survival situations. Why? Because without energy we get caught and eaten, or get diseases and die. *Energy is survival.*

Unlike anaerobic glycolosis, the mitochondria require oxygen to perform their energy magic—the "Chinese Rice Bowl trick" of turning one molecule of glucose into 39 molecules of energy via its two innate pathways. One pathway, known as the Krebs Cycle, derives 36 molecules of energy packets called ATP (Adenosine TriPhosphate).

This is the primary conveyer belt of mitochondrial energy production. Another mitochondrial pathway, called the *electron transport chain* picks up the by-product of glycolosis called *pyruvate*[§], and converts it into three energy packets of ATP provided there is oxygen in the cell to do this, otherwise it will convert to lactic acid and cause sore muscles. Again we see the *Law of Economy* in Nature—the body does not waste resources. The entire mission is to render the most life-energy with the least amount of effort, and the results being the precious packets of energy called ATP.

Mitochondrial production of energy is not really about making "something out of nothing;" it's an amazingly enriching *return on investment* that takes one molecule of glucose and makes 36 molecules of useable, transportable energy. Further, to take a waste product, lactic acid and convert it to a tone[§] called *pyruvate,* and make three more molecules of pure energy ATP, demonstrates how important it is for the cells to generate the energy of Life.

So let's pick up with *Acetyl-CoA* that starts what's known as the Krebs Cycle (citric acid cycle) because here's where the miracle of life-maintenance occurs. As we know, the mitochondria, with the help of various dietary nutrients, all work together to render 36 molecules of energy from one molecule of glucose—provided a person has

Some Food Nutrients Necessary For Mitochondrial Production of ATP
- Vitamins:
  B-1, B-2, B-3, B-5, C,D, E
- Proteins:
  Carnitine, Cysteine, Glutamine Histadine, Glutamic acid, Isoleucine, Methionine, Phenylalanine, Proline, Tyrosine, Valine
- Minerals:
  Iron, Magnesium, Zinc, Phosphorus, Sulfur, Manganese
- Nutrients:
  Lipoic acid, Co-enzyme Q-10

Some Food Nutrients Necessary For Electron Chain Transport Production of ATP
- Vitamins: B-2, B-3, C, K
- Protein:Carnitine
- Minerals: Magnesium, Zinc
- Nutrients: Co-enzyme Q-10

enough oxygen available to the cells. Now that's efficiency! And the waste products of this work are only carbon dioxide (CO_2), which the plants need to breathe, and pure, nascent water (H_2O) because the cellular waste, lactic acid, can be converted to more ATP via the *electron transport chain*. Thus the human body sets the standard for making energy without pollution—a model to which human beings should aspire in our external world!

Kindergarten Nutrition. Now you understand that the production of energy requires a good diet of whole, natural foods—proteins, fats, and carbohydrates that are replete with all their trace minerals and trace nutrients that Nature provides. This means that every time you eat a whole food—raw vegetables, raw seeds, fresh fruit, raw nuts, olives, avocado, etc.—you are getting all the compliments of Nature. When you eat processed foods [white bread, sugar, coffee (heat-altered oils), sodas, pastries, candy, crackers, chips, donuts, etc.] they can choke down your body's energy processes by: 1) being deficient in nutrients, 2) warping the cell membranes with trans-fats and chemicals that cause inflammation, 3) jamming up the cell membranes with toxic food additives, artificial colors, 4) blocking oxygen's access to your mitochondria, and 5) inhibiting your production of Life energy. (But you knew that already, right!)

ATP – the Miracle Molecule of Life-Energy. Now let's take a brief look at this miracle molecule of energy called ATP. As we've discussed, within your cells the mitochondria make the *pure chemical energy of life*—a molecule known as ATP. When your cells are stoked and making energy, there is a more optimal tissue performance that results in more optimal health.

In summary of all that biochemistry is this simple overview. Your body needs fuel for cellular ATP production. α-Glycopeptides are a marvelous, ready fuel source (and so much more) to supply your mitochondria with the fuel to make ATP.

Human beings in optimal health can experience all that life has to offer and better serve their purpose—physically, emotionally, mentally, and spiritually.

Fuel For Life—ATP. To emphasize this point, ATP is the very currency of cellular life—the biochemical-currency upon which your life is founded. When your cells make the right amount of ATP, everything works well "everything" includes your brain, digestion, nerves, metabolism, hormones, muscles, libido, immune system, and your detoxification systems. You name it—if you want it to work better, your cells need to make the right amount of ATP.

If you don't make enough ATP for your cells to function optimally, then there are consequences, and the body's necessary "messengers of consequences" are called "symptoms§" in the English language. If your ATP levels drop below what is required for fundamental life processes, then you die. Thus if you run low on ATP, your body can allow dreaded disease processes to occur – it's the best a body can do under the circumstances. The reason that a poison such as cyanide, is so deadly is because it stops the enzymes and processes that make ATP. It does so by denying oxygen to the cells for mitochondrial function— which results in a quick and dramatic demise.

Practically every cell in our bodies has miniature power plants, called the mitochondria where glucose and other simple sugars mix with oxygen and burn to keep us warm, active and alive. If the fuel mix is correct, it contains a mixture of mostly glucose/ribose, a tiny amount of amino acids and fat, and the right amount of oxygen for proper combustion. When this mixture is present, then the cellular life-fires burn properly, providing stable health and optimal energy. Everything is fine as long as these elements can be maintained.

The Pro-Vita! Plan For Optimal Nutrition
(Tips) 1986

Making ATP for life-processes separates the living from the dead, the healthy from the diseased, the vital from the weak. Making abundant ATP is tantamount to both survival and optimal health.

For an analogy, we know that your car is designed to run on a specific fuel. Whether it's diesel, gasoline, high-octane gasoline, cooking oil, methane, hydrogen, solar, electricity, water, or alcohol; your car will perform its best when given the perfect fuel for which it was designed. When your car has its perfect fuel, it runs smoothly with power to spare. It even has the energy to tow another vehicle. And it's the same with cellular energy in your body.

To complete our biochemistry discourse on energy, ATP has been referred to as "packets of energy." When the body needs energy for a life function, whatever it may be, it releases the energy stored in ATP by splitting that molecule into the combustible and explosive energy molecule called ADP (Adenosine DiPhosphate) and phosphorus. So ATP is the body's currency or wealth of energy, and ADP is the actual spending of that currency for a high quality life experience.

When ATP is reduced to ADP, there is a tiny explosion of phosphorescent light. This is why humans are often called "beings of light." Within our bodies, millions of tiny lights blink on as energy is applied for the body to accomplish its vital functions. People with good cellular energy have glowing personalities!

Different tissues will spend ATP for different functions. The heart will expend it for muscular contractions over and over with every beat. The leg muscles will contract and expand for movement. The kidneys will use it to filter the blood, make hormones, generate ch'i[§], and repair its tissues. The brain will use it for thought. The immune system will use it to make antibodies or kill a threatening pathogen. The intestines will use it to allow the importation of food nutrients. Again, ATP is the universal currency, and ADP is its payload.

ATP and Intestinal Health. Many people know that our health is intimately linked with intestinal bacteria known as "probiotics" or "intestinal flora"—those billions of friendly bacteria that inhabit our gastro-intestinal tracts and protect us from pathogens, help us digest our food, and make nascent B-vitamins for our energy metabolism and nerves. Probiotic florae prevent intestinal inflammation. Intestinal inflammation is much worse than a disease labeled *colitis* or *irritable bowel*. It is a root cause of systemic inflammation which in turn leads to neuro-degenerative diseases via a condition called "leaky gut syndrome", where large molecule food products enter the bloodstream and trigger immunological reactions that can damage the brain, nerves, joints, thyroid, pancreas, arteries, and other tissues.

Few people understand that our intestines are more than a selectively permeable pipe that holds beneficial bacteria and excretes food residues. Our intestines must also have energy so they can function to help our bodies assimilate nutriments.

Most people know that using antibiotics kills both the "good guys'"(beneficial intestinal flora, part of our immune systems) along with the "bad guys" (pathogenic bacteria). If someone requires an antibiotic (a possible sign of a lack of ATP because the cells must signal the immune system, and the immune system requires energy to clone antibodies to fight pathogens), they know to replace the beneficial cultures with broad-spectrum probiotic cultures.

Often people fail to account for the fact that the intestines need ATP energy to perform their specific function of selectively allowing absorption of food nutrients. Many antibiotics and non-steroidal anti-inflammatory drugs disrupt ATP processes as a side-effect. Thus the recipe for restoring gastro-intestinal flora after antibiotic use should include not only probiotics, but also an ATP-process recovery plan such as the α-glycopeptides that we are talking about here if optimal intestinal energy is to be re-instated.

Like your car, your body needs the perfect fuel for which it was designed. And the fact is—you are not getting the proper fuel to your cells, so you really don't know what your body can do regarding your energy, health, and quality of life. This is the dire energy plight of the human condition here at the start of the 21st Century.

Cut To The Chase – Summary #2

1. The three big categories of food—protein, fat, and carbohydrate—can each be rendered into a starter molecule for energy. The human body is designed to survive.

2. Inside the cell, organelles called mitochondria use our food nutrients to produce packets of energy called ATP.

3. ATP is the universal life-currency of health. It is the energy the body needs for thought and actions. ATP is the prime resource for LIFE—including the function and repair of the body in good health.

4. When you have optimal production of ATP, your body can function most optimally. Without adequate production of ATP, your body has an energy crisis that can result in thousands of different diseases, especially what are called the "mitochondrial diseases" which include practically all chronic-degenerative and auto-immune diseases.

5. *α-Glycopeptides* provide your cells a rapidly absorbed, ideal fuel to make ATP. Even more, they provide the peptides that facilitate cell communication and immune system regulation, as well as anthocyanins to boost antioxidant protection.

The Human Energy Crisis. Our car-fuel analogy holds true for human cellular energy combustion. Human beings need the right fuel for their cells, and when the cells have plenty of the proper fuel, they hum along beautifully and serve the body with optimal performance and health, provided we supply it with the nutrients and a lifestyle in accordance with the natural laws of health.

We first need to understand that our current dietary intake is only providing an incomplete fuel and the result is less than optimal performance. On the current Standard American Diet (appropriately abbreviated S.A.D), it's difficult to deliver proper fuel and nutrition to your cells. This is a primary reason that people in the United States suffer such a low state of health and experience such alarming obesity. The USA ranks #1 in obesity of the industrial nations, and #9 in the world after eight tiny island populations where the S.A.D has impacted local cultures as it has in Tonga and other Pacific islands. In overall health, where #1 is the best, the United States ranks at a paltry #55 according to the World Health Organization[3], thus there are 54 other countries that have overall better health. Not a very good score, eh?

Obviously something is majorly wrong with our system of diet and health care. So much so that scientists have labeled the United States as "the sick society." The underlying issue is a lack of ATP production in the cells, and the reasons for that dire energy shortage are legion including: improper farming methods which use only a 3-nutrient fertilizer, and toxic pesticides, as well as food additives, food processing (white flour products, refined sugar, partially-hydrogenated oils, etc.) toxins in the air (automobile exhaust, industrial wastes), gross overuse of prescription drugs, damaged intestinal flora, mercury in dental amalgams and vaccinations. Also there are toxins in municipal

---

3   World Health Organization -- WHO is the directing and coordinating authority for health within the United Nations system. It is responsible for providing leadership on global health matters, shaping the health research agenda, setting norms and standards, articulating evidence-based policy options, providing technical support to countries and monitoring and assessing health trends.

water supplies (chlorine, fluoride, medication residues, chloramines, chemicals). Chronic infections (dysbiosis§, cavitations§), chronic inflammations, radiations from cell phones and microwave towers, also contribute to the all pervading energy crisis. No doubt about it, we live in, and are struggling to adapt to, a hostile universe, and the one most important thing our bodies need to perform optimally is plenty of ATP.

Here in the USA, people gorge themselves on "ghost foods" – foods of empty calories and low nutrition that do not support cellular health, as opposed to many other countries of low health ranking where starvation and epidemic diseases run rampant. But the sad Standard American Diet is proliferated all over the world making for a global, cellular energy crisis. This is why, in my humble opinion, it is virtually impossible to eat right according to your cellular needs if you are not a bit of a "health nut" who includes Nature's wholesome, raw, whole, organic foods in your diet daily.

So many people are completely estranged from the truth that we, as a culture, call people who respect the temple of their bodies and provide Nature's bounty for sustenance as "a bit nutty" e.g. crazy. This cultural bias is part of the inertia human beings must now overcome and their cries of health-degenerative pain are fueling a return to a more healthy diet.

Health Nut. For fun, I'll share with you my definition of a "health nut." In my 40 years of dietary research, I learned that it's what a person does 80% of the time that sets the standard of their nutritional health. Thus if 80% of your diet is based on whole foods from Nature, (mostly raw, organic), salads, fruit, nuts, seeds, and vegetables, then the 20% of dietary indiscretions (a bite of pie, an organic chocolate bar, eating out, eating something someone made for you, etc.) is really no big problem to the body because it's made to handle a certain amount of "junk" under its innate rules of survival. So a health nut is a person who exceeds the 80% rule and is even more fastidious about everything that goes into her/his body. There is certainly nothing wrong with that! So now you know that I'm a bit of a heath nut, but one that takes the 20% of liberties with a relaxed joy. So what most people call a "health nut" is really directed at a person doing what *they* should be doing for energy and freedom from disease. We should save the moniker "health nut" for the healthy, vibrant, person who is waaaay over the top with dietary fastidiousness, and when we say it, we might smile in commiseration for the person who is wise enough to live life in the most optimal nutritional health possible.

So do you have all the energy you need for an optimal life? Consider these questions:

Human Energy Crisis Questionnaire

1. Do you get headaches?

2. Have you had a cold or flu in the past three years?

3. Do you have menstrual symptoms (PMS, irregular, profuse, cramping, clotting)?

4. Wake unrefreshed, without enthusiasm to start the new day?

5. Unable to walk ten miles? (Become too tired?)

6. Do you have hypo or hyper-glycemia (diabetic), or irritable if you miss a meal?

7. Do you have indigestion – heartburn, burping, acid reflux – or other gastro-intestinal symptoms – colitis, irritable bowel, gastritis?

8. Are you often constipated?

9. Are you often chilly – cold hands and feet?

10. Are you foggy headed, forgetful, or lack concentration?

11. Do you have any chronic-degenerative diseases—arthritis, etc.?

12. Are you overweight? (75% of the USA population will be in 2015.)

13. Do you have swollen glands or have intermittent fevers?

14. Do you have elevated cholesterol or blood pressure?

15. Do you have skin problems – pimples, eczema, psoriasis, acne?

16. Do you take any drugs—over the counter or prescription?

17. Do you crave sweets, chocolate, coffee, bread, sodas?

18. Are you tired at the end of a normal day?

19. Do you wish you had more energy to meet the rigors of the day?

20. Do you have health concerns that don't go away or recur frequently?

There are no points to score because every question is reflective of a cellular energy crisis somewhere in your body. I know, it's virtually impossible for you to make it through that questionnaire without checking at least one of the items, but that's the point—we are all caught up in the human energy crisis.

Q. If you have symptoms of a personal energy crisis, what is the number one thing you can do to encourage your body to alleviate the situation?

A. The first thing to do is increase ATP at the cellular level. Taking α-glycopeptides is excellent nutrition for your whole body.

The human energy crisis today is based on the fact that many people are not getting the proper fuel to their mitochondria. The proper fuel is unavailable because of the quality of the diet, lack of exercise, and poor digestion. Also the fuel is blocked from entering the cell by the following causes: the molecules are too large (poor diet and poor digestive breakdown), the cell membrane has other "junk" molecules (pseudo hormones, toxins, chemicals) blocking the entrance pathways, or dehydration (from drinking sodas instead of water), free radical damage to the delicate cell membranes from the oxidation of various toxins and cellular waste products. Most all diseases involve damage from free radicals, and free radicals are the result of 1) acquisition from the environment, 2) lack of cellular ATP energy, 3) lack of antioxidants that protect mitochondrial DNA.

Within many people's bodies, their combustion engines are lined up at the fuel pumps like cars at the gas station during a fuel shortage, but the pumps are not getting the fuel into the gas tank. This inevitably means poor performance of body functions which result in symptoms, pains, low energy, lack of productivity, poor heath and depression. Thus scientists say that a lack of cellular energy is a common denominator in all diseases.

What The Human Energy Crisis Means For Your Health

Neuro-Endocrine Function. When your hypothalamus (part of your brain's regulatory mechanism) perceives that your endocrine glands' mitochondria are not producing enough ATP energy which results in reduced hormone output. It sends a signal to your pituitary gland (the master endocrine gland located in the middle of your brain) to tell your energy glands—thyroid and adrenal glands—to secrete more hormones. This provides your cells with the message to ramp up the energy production, but often the cells cannot respond due to a lack of fuel and lack of oxygen.

To counter the lack of fuel, a person may eat sugar or drink coffee, but such stimulations are but it's not the gentle, sustaining, feel-good energy of ATP; they are the jangle of a caffeine buzz and sugar high that can make you revved up and shaky. Plus the refined sugar starts a disease cycle in the body that can go through hypoglycemia and become diabetes. The coffee and a donut is the wrong way to address fatigue.

Your adrenal glands have access to energy – the small amount of glucose stored in your muscles (legs, arms, heart). Thus, while trying to help you with your energy requirements, accessing muscular glucose actually depletes your energy reserves, and you become more easily fatigued. It's a short-term loan that the body expects to be paid back quickly, except most people's diets do not contain the nutritional materials to pay back that loan. This is a part of what happens with people whose cellular energy declines due to illness, trauma, stress, and all the other reasons cited earlier.

Stimulants Cause Stress. Using coffee (caffeine), sodas, and refined sweets (candy) for energy may help in the short run, but like a loan shark's dollars, you're in big trouble when you can't pay it back. And you can't pay it back unless you address the *cause* of your energy crisis – lack of fuel entering your cells to make ATP.

This is how people become addicted to coffee, sodas, and energy drinks. They provide a metabolic jolt of adrenal-driven energy only to find that later they crash and must renew the loan. The end result is that these drinks create an additional metabolic stress on the body and overall energy depletion – the very thing that doctors say is linked with so many of the modern day diseases – osteoporosis, heart disease, diabetes, and cancer.

The largest user of glucose energy in your body is your brain. Second to the brain are your red blood cells whose job is to carry oxygen to your brain as well as groups of cells throughout your body so the mitochondria can make more energy. (The body teaches us its priorities!) The heart is another big energy user, as is the liver. When your body is in an altered glucose-energy relationship, such as using your thyroid and adrenal glands to force energy availability, the amount of glucose reaching your brain declines resulting in a sugar craving and 'brain fog' that is tantamount to poor health.

When the blood is not carrying enough oxygen, the end product of glycolosis is lactic acid instead of the pyruvate that can be converted to more ATP via the mitochondrial electron transport chain that we've discussed. This also occurs when there is a lack of the B vitamins needed for energy synthesis. B-vitamin deficiency occurs when there is 1) A lack of raw vegetables in the diet, antibiotic damaged intestinal flora (the bacteria make nascent B vitamins, particularly B-12), and from the use of sodas and sweets that rob the body of B Vitamins through an increased rate of urinary excretion. Be advised that if you wake up with stiff and sore muscles and you did not overexert yourself, you are probably lacking in oxygen delivery to your cells, e.g. lacking in exercise.

Excess lactic acid from the loan-shark-approach to energy also stimulates the adrenals to produce the stress hormone cortisol, which leads to further depletion of glucose from the muscles. A cortisol imbalance causes: 1) loss of tissue integrity, 2) depletes serotonin — your feel good neurotransmitter in your brain, 3) fatigue, and 4) abdominal fat storage.

Now you can see that either a person is spiraling upward on the mitochondrial-ATP energy continuum, or spiraling down into disease on the adrenal-cortisol energy loan continuum. We need both processes for survival as they both serve a purpose, but we must return to the feel good, calm, strong, well-being energy of ATP. α-Glycopeptides help the body replenish the mitochondrial ATP energy production and thus serve the body to relieve metabolic stress.

ATP energy is often discerned by a quick mind, creativity, good memory, clear thoughts, and a lack of any nagging fatigue. It's a calm, relaxed feeling based on strength and access to energy when it is needed. An ATP-rich body gets more done!

That Lovin' ATP feeling. We should understand what cellular energy feels like. It's not so much a tangible, jump-up-and-down energy feeling. Instead, it's a deep well-being that let's you know you have plenty of energy to do whatever the day demands, a knowing that you can handle changes in the weather, unexpected work, lending a hand to someone in need, and even jump up and down if you want to. It keeps us feeling terrific, even when there is much physical and mental work to do. For me, it means having plenty of energy after the day's work is done to enjoy a hike or bike ride and still have plenty of energy later.

To emphasize this point—ATP is the potential energy of a large lake that feeds the kinetic energy of a waterfall. Most people know the kinetic energy of an artificially boosted energy from caffeine and sugar, but that is in no way the same as the deep, calm feeling of cellular energy to do all that the body needs to do, plus the reserves on tap for exertion and the demands of life.

Sleep Issues. Some people wake up in the middle of the night and can't get back to sleep. A common reason for this is that lactic acid (a metabolic waste product) builds up when the mitochondria lacks fuel and has difficulty producing ATP. When lactic acid builds up, the body's pH (acid/alkaline balance) shifts to an acidic pH and there is less oxygen available for the body's energy processes that occur during sleep when the body heals and restores tissues. With low oxygen, the body wakes up so the person moves around and breathes in more air. More energy and oxygen contribute to a better functioning brain. This is probably a basis for the many reports of α-glycopeptides helping people sleep.

Further, according to doctors, the lactic acid build up is linked

> I can't believe it! I'm sleeping through the night! I'd tried everything over the past 20 years—melatonin, 5-hydroxy tryptophan, tryptophan, GABA, passion flower, kava, hops, combination homeopathic sleep remedies, yogic exercises, valerian, biofeedback, lavender, lemon balm, California poppy, chamomile, magnesium, relaxation techniques, meditation, white noise – I mean everything. By my third night on α-glycopeptides, I'm sleeping through the night. I know this is the beginning of the end of my deep, deep fatigue. Thank you times a million.
>
> Cass C.

with Chronic Fatigue Syndrome, fibromyalgia, migraine headaches, physical depression, post-partum depression, irregular heartbeat, and diabetes. So it should come as no surprise that there are many reports of α-glycopeptides helping people who are experiencing those "messengers of consequence" conditions. (We will discuss more on fibromyalgia and chronic pain a bit later in this book.)

Next, let's look at the source of α-glycopeptides – a whole food, close to nature, meticulously prepared to support your life processes.

In Praise Of The Elements

Born of Earth, Metal, Water, Wood, and Fire – the source of α-glycopeptides is derived from the heart of a plant that grows, as it's grown for thousands of years, in a remote, protected valley where the *Land* provides nascent *Minerals* and nutrient-rich *Water* that give rise to the *Plants* that thrive in the *Sun*. All the primal elements of life on Earth combine to make one of Nature's great gifts to humankind.

A vitally important foundation of Life on this planet is dependent upon the plants to which our bodies are adapted for sustenance, and in the case of α-glycopeptides, the plants are specially-selected, unique strains of rice.

> I know you said that the glycopeptides I take first thing in the morning were for cellular energy, but already I'm sleeping better (I thought energy would keep me awake?), but I just had my first day without that nagging tension in my shoulders and neck. I feel so much lighter, like a great cloud of oppression is lifting from my shoulders. Oh, I stopped taking [named over the counter analgesic/anti-inflammatory], and my chronic pain is only getting less with each day. This supplement is spot on!
>
> Maria O.

Polypeptides[§] (many peptides) come from the heart of the rice seed (endosperm§) where its nutrients have been formed by the very elements of Life. It's one of Nature's marvelous, sustaining foods—a cellular fuel that imparts the nutrients of the earth (glyconutrients§, essential fats, essential proteins, minerals, vitamins, antioxidants, and other nutrients) rendered from the elements. So here, in the living crucible of Life, begins our story.

It Starts With Rice – Nature's Pure And Simple Sustenance

Unbeknownst to many people in the United States and Europe whose cultures are based upon the "wheat standard," rice is a powerhouse of whole, nascent nutrients that support human health in a multitude of ways. There is a reason why rice is, and has been, the staple food for human health for thousands of years. That reason is just now being discovered, deep within the rice grain's cells, and is launching massive research to discover its applications in natural health as well as in drug-pharmacology.

> "Never, no never does Nature say one thing and wisdom another."
>
> Johann Christolph Frederick von Schuller

Right now, the major pharmaceutical labs are conducting intensive research to figure out how to synthetically manufacture and patent glycopeptides to: 1) provide drugs for a new class of diseases called "mitochondrial diseases," 2) get better uptake of drug medicines, and 3) reduce the devastating side effects and deaths from iatrogenic§ disease (prescription drugs and deadly drug interactions, surgeries and hospital errors). The esteemed health-researcher, Gary Null, cites iatrogenic mishaps as causing 783,936 deaths a year in the United States. So the simple glycopeptides from Nature hold a powerful blessing for humanity through their potential to improve the implementation of prescription medicines as well as improve cellular health via nutritional applications.

α-Glycopeptides To The Rescue. Fortunately, Nature has already provided glycopeptides to humanity, and they are already available in the ready-to-work alpha size – the healing power of Nature for individual use.

Mitochondrial Diseases

- Alzheimer's Dementia
- Arteriosclerosis
- Ataxia
- Atherosclerosis
- Autism
- Blindness (non injury)
- Congestive Heart Disease
- Cancer, metastasis
- Cirrhosis, liver (non-viral, non-alcohol)
- Crohn's Disease
- Deafness (non injury)
- Diabetes, Type 2
- Epilepsy
- Fatigue
- Fibromyalgia
- Hypercholesterolemia
- Hypertension
- Gastrointestinal encephalopathy
- Insulin Resistance
- Irritable Bowel Syndrome
- Kidney failure
- Liver failure
- Lupus, systemic
- Multiple Sclerosis
- Muscular Dystrophy
- Myasthenia Gravis
- Neuropathy
- Obesity
- Parkinson's
- Retinitis Pigmentosa
- Rheumatoid Arthritis
- Strokes
- Wilson's Syndrome
- And many more yet to be listed

The Enzacta[§] Corporation, Spring Park, MN, invests in the research of cross-pollinating strains of rice to improve its nutrition, the construction and operation of highly-specialized, proprietary processing equipment to render viable α-glycopeptides from the rice, and distributes the product for individual use.

Within the rice seeds (endosperm) are the glycopeptide molecules that, when made available for human inner-cell nutrition, unleash the cell's innate vitality to perform its life-affirming processes associated with optimal health. From the bran (outer husk) comes anthocyanins—the antioxidants that help the body prevent and reverse chronic inflammation, as well as other nutrient factors such as IP6 (Inositolhexaphosphate) known to inhibit cancer by removing the proliferative iron molecule necessary for tumor growth. Let's take a look at the source of what many believe to be the most exciting and viable nutritional breakthrough of the 21st Century – rice-derived α-glycopeptides.

Overview. To understand how this one whole food molecule can energize your body and bring the best of health, let's start with a fundamental appreciation for Mother Nature's rice as the source of this new research. A seed of rice provides a tiny amount of these rare and beneficial nutritional molecules that, when carefully rendered from the rice endosperm, are known molecularly as α-glycopeptides.

This is not your store-bought or restaurant rice. This is naturally-grown (no chemicals or pesticides), special strains of 'super rice' that are rich in beneficial sugars and proteins – in this case, an array of the α-glycopeptides that the body uses for energy and healing. This amazing molecule contains and transports the very polysaccharides§ (necessary and vital carbohydrate chains) and polypeptides (simple and essential amino acids). These nutrients are of primary importance for the building of tissue, construction of hormones and immunoglobins, repair of DNA, strengthening of the bone matrix, and are a sustaining nourishment for the most basic unit and building block of life —the cell.

> We live and die at the cellular level. All nutrition must be cellular nutrition to impact human health.
>
> Dr. Jack Tips,
> The Pro-Vita! Plan for Optimal Nutrition

Fibromyalgia / Chronic Fatigue Syndrome. One of the first health issues to reveal the pains associated with a lack of cellular energy was labeled *fibromyalgia* by medicine. After many years of claiming, "it's all in your head," and patients being prescribed dangerous antidepressant drugs, researchers found that the chronic pain and debility of fibromyalgia occurred in people who have low levels of cellular ATP production—most likely due to inflammatory damage to the cell membranes and to the mitochondria themselves. With the lower level of cellular energy, they found that the cells could not receive communications (hormone-directives from insulin, estrogen, testosterone, progesterone, thyroxin, etc.), lacked adequate oxygenation, and failed to properly dispose of metabolic wastes due to alterations in their cellular membranes. Thus the body cries out in pain at the dire lack of cellular ATP energy.

Further, many chronic pain sufferers are locked into an inflammatory, self-perpetuating cycle called the Tenth Paradigm[§] of Disease—the "no/onoo" nitric acid/peroxynitrate cascade of localized free-radical induced pain. Their bodies do not produce enough antioxidants to quench the pain/inflammation processes, and so the pain becomes perpetual. The cells' ability to make its regulatory antioxidant molecules is dependent on ATP.

> I find it hard to believe—after my entire adult life has revolved around not having enough energy to do what I need to do everyday such as raising children, preparing meals, maintaining a home, doing things with my husband—that one supplement (α-glycopeptides) is the answer. I don't know whether to laugh or cry, so I'm doing both. If this incredible energy improvement continues, this is the answer to the life I've always wanted to live.
>
> Marcie M.

Eight Essential Sugars? **Not Really.** Researchers have published that our cells need *eight essential sugars* to perform properly. While educating people about an important aspect of nutrition—that there are *healing sugars* and thus not all sugars are "bad," and that there are vitally beneficial sugar molecules that our diets lack, the label "*eight essential sugars*" is not quite accurate. In fact, it's blatantly incorrect.

You see, an *essential nutrient* is one that must be acquired through food. It must be ingested. The body cannot make it from other nutrients and must receive it from the diet. Thus we inherit the need to eat food to maintain life.

We know there are eight essential proteins that must come from diet: *Isoleucine*, *Leucine*, *Lysine*, *Methionine*, *Phenylalanine*, *Threonine*, *Tryptophan* and *Valine*. We know there are two essential fatty acids we acquire through diet: *alpha linolenic acid* (Omega Three), and *linoleic acid* (Omega Six). Also Vitamin C is essential because the human body does not make it, whereas many animals' bodies do make it.

The touted *eight sugars*, while important, can be synthesized in the body with work. Thus they are "important" but not *essential*. We will not perpetuate that misnomer by saying that certain sugars are essential.

Further, our bodies can synthesize sugars, e.g. glucose, from our fat deposits (*ketogenesis*) and from our protein deposits (muscles and tissues via *catabolism*[§].) To do so, the body breaks down fat (ketosis[§]) and muscle (protein catabolism) to render the sugar energy needed for survival, and this is a less than optimal process.

Many people are familiar with low-carb weight-loss plans that "burn fat" to make ketones for energy, often at the expense of losing muscle mass as well as activating the body's rebound effect know as "yoyo-ing." The point here is to illustrate that our bodies have back up systems for survival.

Now that we have correct terminology, we can discuss one of the important, beneficial sugars.

Here's an alarming statistic. According to many nutritionists, most people only get two of the important sugars dietarily, leaving many critically vital life processes unaddressed or addressed on a catch-as-catch-can basis. When the body has to work to manufacture or convert a molecule, as opposed to getting it delivered dietarily, that work represents a "stress" or energy expenditure that unnecessarily uses important resources—ATP energy. Over time, this expends unnecessary energy and takes a toll on health.

Remember that the fundamental equation of nutrition is this: does your food provide your body more energy than it utilizes to process the food? If you are "in the red" nutritionally (meaning that you eat the sad Standard American Diet) and expend more energy digesting, absorbing, assimilating, humanizing, and disposing of metabolic wastes, then you are creating a human energy crisis and wasting your precious ATP. Ultimately this can lead to disease. If however, your dietary practice provides more energy than you expend in rendering those molecules, then you are on the positive continuum of feeling good, avoiding disease processes, and being vital and youthful. Energy and the acquisition of nutrients (essential and otherwise) is the expressed purpose of nutrition. Knowing that, you can understand the aphorism: *Do you live to eat or eat to live?*

Here is a chart of information about the eight important sugars that your body needs to have and use every day:

Nutritional Sugars	Food Sources
Glucose	Nearly all ripe fruits and vegetables. This sugar is overly abundant in most diets. Honey, grape, banana, mango, cherries, strawberry, cocoa, aloe vera, licorice, sarsaparilla, hawthorn, garlic, echinacea, kelp.
Galactose	Dairy products, fenugreek, kelp, apple pectin, apples, apricot, banana, blackberries, cherries, cranberries, currants, dates, grapes, kiwi fruit, mango, orange, nectarine, peach, pear, pineapple, plums, prunes, raspberries, rhubarb, strawberries, passion fruit, echinacea, boswellia, chestnuts, broccoli, Brussels sprouts, avocado, cabbage, carrot, cauliflower, celery, cucumber, potato, eggplant, tomatoes, leeks, asparagus, lettuce, green beans, mushrooms, beetroot, onions, parsnip, green peas, pumpkin, spinach.

Nutritional Sugars	Food Sources
Mannose	Aloe vera (acemannan—a chain of mannose molecules), kelp, shiitake mushroom, ground fenugreek, carob gum, guar gum, black currants, red currants, gooseberries, green beans, capsicum, cabbage, eggplant, tomatoes, turnip. Vary rare in the Standard American Diet.
Fucose	Kelp, wakame seaweed, brewers yeast. Also very rare in the S.A.D.
Xylose	Kelp, ground psyllium seeds, guava, pears, blackberries, loganberries, raspberries, aloe vera, echinacea, boswellia, broccoli, spinach, eggplant, peas, green beans, okra, cabbage, corn.
N-acetyl glucosamine	Shiitake mushroom, shark cartilage, beef cartilage, glucosamine sulfate.
N-acetylgalactosamine	Shark cartilage, beef cartilage, chondroitin sulphate, red algae called Dumontiaceae. Absent from the S.A.D.
N-acetylneuraminic acid	Whey protein concentrates or isolate, chicken eggs.

An important consideration regarding the eight important sugars is that in our modern diet, we are only assimilating the first two – glucose and galactose in a quantity to support the body's needs. The other six sugars are rare, damaged in food processing, inhibited by pesticides and food additives, or simply not put on the table. And this is a huge concern for people desiring optimal health through nutrition.

The point here is that the "glyco" molecule portion of the α-glycopeptides is comprised of important sugars often referred to as "healing sugars" and in their own right serve the body in many capacities (such as tissue healing, pain reduction, immunity), as well as providing molecules for the mitochondria to make ATP.

Rice provides this much-needed nutritional glyco-molecule (*glycopeptides*), and provides it in greater abundance than other foods (which may have other virtues and detriments), so rice is the source of the nutritional benefits we are discussing. A simple technology— hydrolyzation§ (water process with pressure) and fine (alpha), precision milling (to a billionth of a unit and smaller) renders the concentrated *α-glycopeptide* molecules while retaining their integrity so they can be taken as a simple dietary supplement.

Please note that eating table rice will not provide the necessary α-glycopeptides for accomplishing a quick solution to the human energy crisis – table rice comes from other strains of rice, does not provide enough molecules, and is not easily rendered into the alpha state by most people's digestive processes without significant ATP and enzyme expenditure.

What the body does with α-glycopeptide molecules, for many people, is nothing short of miraculous. The miracle is really fundamental nutrition at the cellular level. It's simply re-engaging the basic, cellular health processes that people inevitably lack if they are tired or manifesting various symptoms of poor health.

> "So eat always from the table of God: the fruits of the trees, the grain and grasses of the field, the milk of beasts, and the honey of bees."
>
> words attributed to Jesus reported in the Essene Gospel of Peace

One could surmise that so many of our symptoms and diseases are simply the result of fuel-starved cells that have become congested with the residues of an unnatural diet coupled with the toxins and chemicals enshrouding the Earth today. Let's take a quick look at rice so that you can ascertain for yourself if nutritional α-glycopeptides holds the key to your nutritional health and well-being.

A Brief History of Rice

Basic, Staple Nutrition. Rice is certainly one of the most important foods produced by the Earth. Today, half of the world's people thrive on rice as their staple food, the majority of which is consumed in Asia where each person eats 200 – 480 pounds a year. Some three billion people are completely dependent upon rice for sustenance. Statistically, people who use rice as a dietary foundation have not exhibited high rates of the two leading disease causes of death – cancer, and heart disease, (iatrogenic disease excepted).

Records of rice cultivation in China date back 4,000 years, and records of cultivation in India date back 3000 years. In the ancient Chinese language, the words for "agriculture" and for "rice" are synonymous, indicating that rice was already the staple crop at the time the language was taking form. In several Asian languages the words for "rice" and "food" are identical.

> "Rice is the best, the most nutritive and unquestionably the most widespread staple in the world."
>
> Escoffier

So rice is an ancient food to which the human genome is well adapted. This means that it is more than a basic survival food; it is a basic food for health. Human adaptation to rice means that it can easily be digested and assimilated by the body, and even more importantly, rice-nutrients (starches, proteins, vitamins, minerals, fats) are genetically adapted to be accepted by the body's cells and generally do not trigger unwanted immunological responses. More than basic survival, rice brings to the cells a foundational array of nutrients and thus is a basic staple of many people's health. Rice contains glycopeptides for energy, fatty acids for cell membrane integrity, cyanins and antioxidants, proteins to transport nutrients throughout the cell's interior terrain.

Rice is Gluten§ Free. One of the reasons that rice is such a marvelous food is that it is hypoallergenic. It does not contain the highly allergenic protein, *gluten*, which other grains—wheat, rye, oats and barley—contain. Some grains, such as wheat, contain allergenic gluten molecules that are often linked with chronic inflammatory processes. So rice is a leading "gluten-free" grain along with corn, (though for people of European descent, corn can contain other compounds that cause an allergy reaction.) Most humans are genetically well adapted to rice nutrition.

Of course the rice to which our human genome is beautifully adapted is Nature's rice and NOT genetically-modified (GM) rice where the rice's genetics have been spliced and tampered with, viruses added, and a product created that is estranged from what our bodies can properly use.

> "With coarse rice to eat, with water to drink, and my bent arm for a pillow—I have still joy in the midst of these things."
>
> Confucius

Rice Nutrition. People wanting the best nutrition from dietary rice often find that a whole-grain rice contains the best vitamins (thiamin, riboflavin, biotin, niacin, folate), minerals (phosphorus, calcium, potassium, beneficial sodium, magnesium, zinc, iron), essential fats (omega three, gamma oryzanol—a natural antioxidant), enzymes (lipase—that digests its unique fatty acids), proteins (19 amino acids), and other nutriments.

Rice And Human Nutrition. If there is a shortcoming of rice's nutrition profile, it lacks the essential amino acid, *lysine*, and has only a small amount of the essential amino acid, *threonine*. Essential amino acids, as we've discussed, are those that must come from dietary intake,

> "God, in His infinite wisdom, neglected nothing, and if we would eat our food without destroying its life giving elements, it would meet all requirements of the body."
>
> Jethro Kloss, Author of Back To Eden

and non-essential amino acids are those that the body can construct from other amino acids if needed. Historically, rice dishes in the East were, and still are, often accompanied by other proteins such as miso (fermented soy) or other beans, or fish-stock, both of which contain lysine and threonine. Thus the combination provides a full array of the essential amino acids. For this reason, ancient peoples instinctively endeavored to not just live on rice exclusively, but mixed it with fish, sea vegetation, meat, vegetables, and other foods to compliment rice's nutritional profile.

No one food has all the nutrients for human health. Breast milk is Nature's perfect food (provided the diet is optimal and the mom isn't stressed) for infant adaption, growth and survival until the natural weaning time. Human nutrition requires a variety of foods to cover the wide range of needed nutrients in proper quantities.

To complete rice's nutritional profile, in processing one of the two available forms of α-glycopeptides (marketed under the name PXP-Forte®)—a small amount (apx. 1%) of the natural health food, spirulina (65-73% nascent protein) is added. Spirulina contains all 21 amino acids as well as Vitamins, B-1, B-2, B-3, B-6, B-9, B-12, and essential fatty acids such as Gamma-lenolenic acid (GLA), alpha-linolenic acid (ALA), lenoleic acid (LA), eicosapentaenoic acid (EPA), docosahexaenoic acid (DHA), and arachadonic acid (AA), chlorophyll, and a rich source of trace minerals and other nutrients such as antioxidants. Thus the resulting α-glycopeptide product presents a complete and far better balanced nutrition profile than rice by itself.

There is also a second form of α-glycopeptides now on the market, a product containing between two and six times more α-glycopeptides (depending upon which types of α-glycopeptide molecules are counted) than the "Forte" version. Its trade name is PXP-Royale®. The source of this royal version comes from an ancient strain of purple rice improved through successful cross-pollination. Known in China as "forbidden rice" because it was for the exclusive use of the Emperor and his guards, the resulting rice has a greatly enhanced nutritional profile, particularly in its protein and antioxidant content. The Thai government has labeled this exciting new species of rice, "Medical Rice." Because of its rich proteins, it is not necessary to enhance this rice with spirulina to render the nutritional peptide molecules and antioxidants such as *super oxide dismustase* and *anthocyanins*.

Thus, the marketed form of α-glycopeptides provide a cornucopia of essential nutrients – essential proteins, essential fatty acids, and important sugars, and features important nutrients that many people's diets lack.

40,000 Strains Of Rice. Over thousands of years, different strains of rice have appeared and become established as important to human nutritional health, often due to careful breeding as well as the plants' innate adaptations to different climates and soils around the world.

For thousands of years, farmers have been cultivating and breeding rice by cross-pollination (a natural method) to improve its nutritional viability and resistance to pests. Recently, modern plant breeders are seeking to improve the ability of rice to defend itself against diseases. More and more, genetic engineering is being used to achieve breeding objectives that are NOT health or nutritional objectives.

Genetic modification (GM) of a food molecule results in a molecular structure that is not compatible with the body's metabolism and is recognized as xenobiotic by the body's innate intelligence (molecular lock and key processes)—often causing inflammation and immune reactions. Genetically Modified foods are not safe for human health because the modifications were not selected by Nature, whereas cross-pollination methods allow Nature to have a say in the traits elicited.

Genetically Modified Rice = Grave Danger. Genetically Modified (GM) rice is now on its way to fields in several countries and poses a severe threat to Nature's design. Most GM research is aimed at making the rice immune to toxic pesticides so that farmers can add pesticides, fungicides, and herbicides to the irrigation systems or spray on the crops so they can grow without threat. (If a bug is too smart to eat it, why do we think it's good for humans?)

Unfortunately, these altered rices, lock the farmer into a relationship with the pesticide-selling, seed-selling companies because the seeds are sterile. Thus they must buy new seeds and more pesticides regularly from a monopoly-goaled vendor. Greedy corporations are trying to control the world through food.

> "Food is no less a weapon than tanks, guns, and planes."
>
> Franklin D. Roosevelt

Nutritionally, the GM crops do not properly support human nutrition as their molecular composition is altered and can include pesticides that interfere with human health and cellular uptake of nutrition. Further, GM strains can spread their genetics to natural strains thus adulterating and ruining the entire human food supply. This is a very dangerous activity that is occurring now.

When the plant genetics are altered by Science via x-rays, nuclear radiation, and viruses, to accomplish the alterations, instead of allowing Nature to work, the resulting food contains altered molecules that the human body may not recognize or utilize in the same way that the food was used over thousands of years. Thus the "new foods" are not compatible with the human genome. This can cause allergies as happened in the case of wheat, rape seed (canola®), and other food products, or cellular confusions that can result in auto-immune diseases. In test crops, the GM food has killed the animals that ate it. Further, genetically-modified plants can adulterate the entire global food supply as their pollens are carried to other fields both near and far. These are just some of the concerns that some scientists present regarding genetically-modified crops.

Not Nanotechnology[§]. Fine milling and hydrolyzation is not GM, and it's not "Nanotechnology" though it does render the tiny molecules.

While we're on this subject, the "exceedingly fine" milling of the rice for cellular uptake is a simple, proprietary process. It's NOT to be associated with "nanotechnology" where researchers are manipulating matter at the molecular level and introducing altered plastics and fibers into the marketplace and into our bodies via cosmetics. Nor is the milling a "synthetic biology."

The concern with science's new, man-made nano-molecules is that, for instance, a baby toy made with nano-technology particles can have its xenobiotic§ molecules absorb right through the baby's skin where they then interact with the cells causing errant cellular behaviors such as the inability to properly utilize hormone messengers.

> The rice used to produce the α-glycopeptides are stringently protected by the Thai government, and no GM rice is used whatsoever.

Thus the concern regarding "nanotechnology" is that science is altering Nature's molecules and the new, altered molecules can be very toxic to the body setting off immune reactions, auto-immune diseases, and death. Obviously nanotechnology is a two-edged sword. Science can create new plastics, liquid glass, and drug delivery systems to help humankind. However, without respect for Nature and understanding Natural Law, science most often creates molecules that cause major health concerns when they interact with the human genome. An example is the way asbestos is the cause of mesothelioma cancer, except nano-molecules can get inside our cells.

Again, the exceedingly fine milling of the rice for nutritional α-glycopeptides does not alter Nature's rice genome. It simply renders a completely assimilable, "nano-sized" cellular food—one that the cells greatly appreciate and use to improve a person's nutritional health.

Superior, Natural Rice. Some rice strains have a higher essential fat and protein content, others have a higher complex carbohydrate value as established by Nature. The classification of rice strains that are referred to in the industry as "miracle rice" have both a higher glycan (carbohydrates) and a higher protein content than other rice strains. Each strain has its virtues, and the strains that are used to produce α-glycopeptides are specially selected to render the α-glycopeptides of this book's interest.

Kaizen (Change For The Better). Many scientists and researchers around the world work with natural methods (cross pollination) to improve the nutritional profile of strains of rice. Periodically, new strains of rice with a higher nutritional profile are rendered, thus the sources of the α-glycopeptide product gets better and better over time. This ensures that the natural nutritional benefits of supplemental α-glycopeptides increase with a dedication to *kaizen* (constant and never-ending improvement.) On August 6, 2010, the PXP-Royale was introduced after four years of research including field-testing in an hospital environment, and provides an upgraded version of α-glycopeptides to the world.

Glycopeptides & The Nobel Prize. Equally exciting, and important to know, is that the last four Nobel Prizes in Physiology and Medicine were awarded to researchers regarding glycopeptides. Further, specifically cited in the Massachusetts Institute of Technology Review's article called *The 10 Emerging Technologies That Will Change The World*, one of those 10 is research on the polysaccharide/polypeptides (glycopeptides) making them "very

"Rice is a beautiful food. It is beautiful when it grows, precision rows of sparkling green stalks shooting up to reach the hot summer sun. It is beautiful when harvested, autumn gold sheaves piled on diked, patchwork paddies. It is beautiful when, once threshed, it enters granary bins like a (flood) of tiny seed-pearls. It is beautiful when cooked by a practiced hand, pure white and sweetly fragrant."

Shizuo Tsuji

important molecules."

Glycopeptides and Research. People often ask, "With something this exciting, are there any research studies proving what you're saying?" Yes, indeed there are. I like to read research studies, but I'm personally not very trusting about them, whatever they say, because often in the case of drug testing, the funding comes from the pharmaceutical company wanting to sell the drug, often the conclusions are predetermined, and the research study is designed to prove the points that the manufacturer wants.

Also, if you don't know as much as the researchers, you may miss how research studies become skewed. This recently happened with a research study on Vitamin E where the ulterior motive was to discredit Vitamin E, so the study was set up to use a synthetic form of Vitamin E (derived from mothballs, acetone, and sulfuric acid — e.g. photography by-product chemicals) instead of the plant form of Vitamin E from Nature. A similar study occurred with the herb Echinacea where the study only used an isolated compound instead of the whole plant and used a dose that was too low in order to discredit the herb's reputed effectiveness regarding the immune system.

Emory University Study. Now on the more positive side of research studies, and free from shenanigans, there was an Emory University study done by Dr. Sayan Sawatsri, M.D. and Wanphen Yankunthong, M. Sc. (Research assistant, Department of Obstetrics and Gynecology, Bangkok, Thailand) regarding the neuro-protective aspect of α-glycopeptides.

Here, verbatim, are their published results: *"Results of these analysis demonstrated that Enzacta glycopeptides significantly decreased neuronal cell death, a cellular marker of memory formation. Dose response analysis indicated that the lowest effective concentration of PXP exerted the minimal neurotrophic effect. Result of neuro-protection studies demonstrated the PXP induced highly significant neuro-protection against beta-amyloid, hydrogen peroxide, glutamate-induced toxicity."*

Here, verbatim, is their conclusion: *"Enzacta's glycopeptides induced cellular markers of memory function in neurons critical to memory and vulnerable to negative effects of aging, cellular degeneration and [named specific] disease. Results of the current study could demonstrate the cellular mechanism of cognitive function and a possible intervention in [named specific] disease."*

Cho Ray Hospital Study. From the Vietnamese Ministry of Health and Cho Ray Hospital comes another study—a 28-page document with photos—that was conducted by the hospital staff as the test subjects and control group.

Here, verbatim, is their published conclusion: *The use of this "Proprietary Enzacta Glycopeptide" natural food supplement powder, as part of an overall diet, proved to be highly successful in lowering the overall risk factors associated with Coronary Heart Disease (CHD) through a significant increase in HDL-C, Apo A-1, while concurrently obtaining reduction in LDL-C.*

Cut To The Chase – Summary #3

We all need more cellular energy to handle the modern day stressors – the polluted environment and pace of life. Those who provide their bodies a nutritional foundation of cellular energy (α-glycopeptides) are more adaptable and maintain better health.

- Humanity is experiencing life energy crisis at the cellular level resulting in practically every "no known cause, no known cure", chronic, degenerative disease.

- ATP is the cell's chemical energy of life and can serve to correct the Human Energy Crisis.

- Naturally grown (no pesticides, no synthetics), naturally cross-pollinated (no GM, no synthetic biology) rice is the source of nutritional a-glycopeptides.

- Two studies have already shown the efficacy of a-glycopeptides.

- No such thing as eight "essential" sugars because one sugar molecule can be converted to the others within the body. There are eight important sugars for human nutrition known at this time.

- GM (genetically modified) foods are a threat to human health.

- Nanotechnology poses threats to human health.

- α-Glycopeptides are NOT GM, and NOT nanotechnology or synthetic biology.

α-Glycopeptides are a proven method to help people solve their life-energy crises, and restore their body's innate life processes.

The Plight of the Cell

In a perfect, unpolluted world, a person would simply eat rice and derive a tiny amount of α-glycopeptides from normal digestion, assimilation, and utilization of the food. However today, nutrient uptake is inhibited for three reasons: 1) poor digestion, 2) incapacitated cell membranes that are less able to facilitate the induction of nutrition through the cell wall, and 3) a high stress world. Stress diminishes digestion via the adrenal stress hormones (cortisol, epinephrine, and norepinephrine), and interferes with the liver's humanization[§] of food.

Most people today have impaired digestive systems so they are not able to assimilate as much nutrition as they are eating. There are many reasons for this embraced by the natural health doctors—poor food choices, food combinations that inhibit enzymes, snacking on junk foods, stress, overeating, cooking and overcooking, intestinal dysbiosis and inflammation from antibiotic use, not chewing properly, etc.

It's not what you eat but what your cells can absorb and utilize that is the true measure of your nutritional status.

The only true measure of nutrition is what the human cell can accept and utilize to serve its life processes – production of ATP (energy), repair and maintenance of cellular integrity, resistance to invading micro-organisms, performance of its purpose (tissue function), and the excretion of metabolic wastes. These fundamental processes must be operative for the cell to be a productive unit of the human life experience. Thus like a person's home, the cell welcomes friends, repels enemies, and seeks optimal function of its inherent life processes. Thus "true nutrition" is not a measure of calories or "fortified" synthetic vitamins, or anything put on a product label, it is simply a measure of what aids the impeccable performance of the cell.

Dr. Jack Tips, lecture in Coolangatta, Australia, 2008

The second reason explains why people often take vitamin supplements — even natural supplements (as opposed to U.S. pharmacopeal neutraceuticals) and do not derive much benefit. The cells never receive the nutritional factors through their membranes and their lymphatic systems are congested with large molecule proteins and waste products. Damage of the cell membrane by free radicals makes the cell more and more susceptible to toxins and thus function at a much lower level. Low cellular function is tantamount to disease.

Once we understand that energy is the critical factor, then we can see how α-glycopeptides are **the number one most important supplement a person can take,** because they are ready for quick induction into the cell where they help create the energy that the cell needs to repair itself and its membrane.

Before we touch briefly on the cell membrane and induction of nutrients into the cell, let's take a quick Digestive Evaluation. Many people find that when starting to take α-glycopeptides, they work in the body where they are needed most as defined by the body's innate intelligence. For many people, α-glycopeptides are most needed by their gastro-intestinal tracts, and so it all starts with improving digestion. Without strong digestion, the body never gets all the food-nutrients it needs. This is why many of the great nutritionists such as Dr. Bernard Jensen and Dr. Norman Walker used phrases such as, "Disease begins on your plate," or "Disease begins in your stomach." They are referring to the supreme importance of having a strong digestive system so your body can use the products of the Earth for sustenance.

Here is a quick overview evaluation of your digestion.

How's Your Digestion?

Circle 'Yes,' or 'No,' or the number that best reflects the intensity of each symptom.

0= never. 1=seldom. 2=occasional. 3=often.

Low Acidity

1. Indigestion 0 1 2 3
2. Abdominal bloating 0 1 2 3
3. Feel too full after eating 0 1 2 3
4. Constipation 0 1 2 3
5. Belching/Burping 0 1 2 3
6. Diminished appetite 0 1 2 3
7. Stomach growls/gurgles 0 1 2 3
8. Any known food allergies? .... No Yes

High Acidity

9. Stomach pains just before or after meals 0 1 2 3
10. Stomach pains with no apparent reason 0 1 2 3
11. Stomach pain relieved by carbonated drinks 0 1 2 3
12. Stomach pain relieved by milk/cream 0 1 2 3
13. Emotional upset causes stomach pain 0 1 2 3
14. Heartburn immediately after meals 0 1 2 3
15. Constant need for antacids 0 1 2 3
16. "Butterfly feeling" in stomach 0 1 2 3
17. Family history of ulcer/gastritis? .... No Yes
18. Ulcer (pain) in the past year? .... No Yes

19. Current ulcer? .... No Yes

20. Very dark or black stool? .... No Yes

21. Hot/spicy food causes stomach irritation? .... No Yes

Each point or 'yes' answer reveals a situation that your body can improve nutritionally. Many people report that α-glycopeptides feel good in the tummy and helps their bodies digest better. People scoring more than 12 points, or having points in 5 of the 21 questions should endeavor to improve their digestion immediately. As you'll learn in this material, α-glycopeptides are a great place to start. Taking enzymes can also help give the digestion a rest so it can repair its processes.

The Plight of the Cell Continues. Let's continue with our discussion about the plight of the cells. It's important to understand that whatever nutrition we consume, it absolutely must be taken into the cells for their use if we are to sustain life and experience optimal health.

> "One-quarter of what you eat keeps you alive. The other three-quarters keeps your doctor alive."
>
> (Hieroglyph found in an ancient Egyptian tomb.)

Hormone Health. Many people's cell membranes are inhibited from the proper uptake of nutrition and hormones. The cells' receptor sites are not functioning properly. This is seen by the pandemic blood sugar distress called "*insulin resistance,*" as well as hormonal failures such as "*thyroxin resistance*" where the cells do not properly respond to the thyroid's commands, and "*leptin[§]-resistance*"—all leading contributors to obesity. Further, much of what is called "menstrual distress" and menopause symptoms are not so much the lack or excess of the glands' hormone output, but the resistance of the cells to respond to the neuro-endocrine hormone messengers that govern the proper release of female hormones into the blood stream. This is all coupled with the individual cells not being receptive to the hormones once they are released into the bloodstream.

Cellular Failure To Communicate. For example, if the estrogen-receptors on the cell membranes are occupied with pseudo estrogens from plastic bottles and tin can liners, or other estrogenic compounds (pesticides, hormones in commercial milk, synthetic hormones in municipal tap water from the recycled urination from the women on synthetic estrogen replacement therapy,) then the body's own processes become confused and symptoms result.

> Hormonal issues from pre-menstrual mood changes to dread diseases are really about the cell membranes and not so much about the producing gland (tumors and reversed hormones excepted.) The body's prime directive is to do what it thinks is right for survival. If the body is found doing something wrong hormonally, it's probably an issue of the receiving cell's membrane resisting the hormonal messenger.
>
> Dr. Jack Tips, Neuro-Endocrinology & You

More specifically, the hypothalamus (brain) tells the pituitary (master gland) to message the ovaries (functional glands) — or in the case of post-menopause, tells the adrenals (functional glands), and fat cells — to release estrogen (hormone), so estrogen is released. But the target cell's estrogen receptor sites are already occupied with non-functional, toxic, pseudo hormones; so the released hormones have no place to go. The appropriate cells never get the message. If the estrogens over-stimulate cellular responses in the breasts or uterus, then estrogenic pathologies can develop. Taking an anti-estrogenic drug is only "killing the messenger" and fails to address the cause of the problem (which is not estrogen) but with the hormone resistance at the cellular level. What we have here is a failure to communicate!

One wonderful aspect of increasing cellular ATP production with α-glycopeptides as a source of fuel, beyond the marvelous ability of α-glycopeptides to get right into the cell, is when the cells have energy, they automatically rev up their ability to burn up toxins and create new locations for hormone receptors that allow the hormone messengers to enter the cell. Thus, gently and effectively the cells reclaim their innate health and optimal function.

The Resistance Movement. Insulin resistance, thyroxin resistance, estrogen resistance, leptin resistance, testosterone resistance, progesterone resistance.

The messengers are at the gate, but the drawbridge is pulled up and the messengers are not getting across the moat to tell the king and queen what's going on.

Simply put, α-glycopeptides are wholeheartedly embraced and eagerly accepted into the cell where they improve the production of cellular energy. When the cell has more bio-available fuel, it has more life! With more fuel, it produces more ATP, so that the miracles of life occur including energy generation, repair of broken DNA, strengthening of bones and muscles, repair of the cell membranes, improvements in cellular immunity, detoxification of metabolic and xenobiotic wastes, restoration of healthy metabolic functions, improvements in the nerves and nerve sheaths, and engagement of healthy reproduction processes for a future life of good health.

Once again, a person cannot eat rice and gain the benefits of ample α-glycopeptides. No way. They just

> Fact: It takes 100 pounds of rice to produce 1 pound of α-glycopeptides.

can't eat and digest enough to get the mass action needed to revitalize the cells in their current energy crisis. Thankfully there is the proper use of technology. The ultra-fine milling/hydrolyzation process is necessary to overcome the same two reasons that people have poor cellular uptake of nutrition—1) overcome impaired digestive processes, 2) get through impaired cell membranes so the mitochondria can create the energy of life, ATP, and thus start the processes necessary for regaining and realizing a more optimal state of health.

Alpha, Beta Cellular Nutrition—Size Matters. Cells cannot accept molecules that are larger than the appropriate size that we designate as α – "alpha" size. This accounts for why, historically, many people who expected better results from beta-glucans (mushrooms, aloe vera) were disappointed. Beta sized molecules are too large to pass into the cell, but instead they can serve the cell if they attach to the cell membrane. Thus there is a valuable health benefit to beta-glucans, and some can be reduced to alpha size by the expenditure of ATP via the cell's "active transport" system. In this book we are talking about true nutrition for the inner cell—alpha glucans (glycans), e.g. α-glycopeptides.

One of the primary purposes of digestive enzymes is to reduce food substances to the *alpha* molecular size so they are absorbable through the cell membrane. Think of the screen on your window. It keeps out birds and bugs, but it won't keep out dust and viruses. To pass through the screen, the item must be smaller than the holes in the screen. But in the case of the human cell, the cell membrane is not a screen, it is an intelligent, selective, living surface that chooses to "lower the drawbridge" and receive nutrition and messengers when it deems it is right and necessary—and doing this often requires ATP, carrier molecules, enzymes, and electrical conductivity.

The window screen analogy is a bit oversimplified because in the body, the cell membrane is an independent tissue with innate intelligence

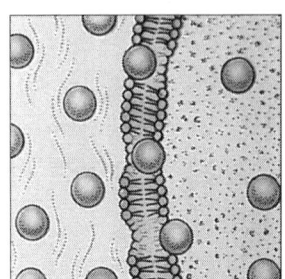

and ability to adapt, change, and open new portals, but it serves our explanation here. Passage through the cell wall portals (embedded glycopeptide) is dependent upon electric charge and carrier molecules of which many are peptides. (Proper function of the intelligence is dependent upon proper nutrition and cellular energy.)

Actually the pH of the extracellular matrix, electrical conductivity (ion exchange), and hydrophobic (water repelling vs water embracing) qualities of a molecule also govern what can be absorbed into the cell. The body has a perfect system. It's only in the past 150 years that humanity has inadvertently fouled it up.

But first, the cell must be receptive and there's nothing like fueling the cell to turn on the system! Once performing optimally, the active cell helps control its environment, and all the other life processes can more easily occur such as the ability to detoxify and the ability to reproduce a healthy, effective cell. So the tipping point of therapeutic leverage is getting fuel to the mitochondria, and that's exactly what α-glycopeptides do.

α-Glycopeptides – The Ultimate "Anti-Aging" Supplement. To emphasize a subtle point, an energized cell with active mitochondria, performs better. One of your cells' functions is reproduction. The quality of the parent cell determines the quality of the offspring. If the parent cell is healthy, then the nucleo-peptides and ATP-generated enzymes that repair damaged DNA (your genetic code) are available for cellular health.

If the cell is sluggish (lacks glycopeptide portals), diseased, and damaged by free radicals, then the offspring cell is not as healthy and viable as it could be. Since α-glycopeptides support the parent cell with energy and anthocyanins (antioxidants), they also support the quality of the offspring. When your body is reproducing healthy cells, it's called "anti-aging" in our modern, confrontational vernacular.

Savvy women should consider the role that α-glycopeptides can play during pregnancy when a constant energy supply is being tapped to create the new life developing via multiplication and replication of cells.

We really don't have to fight aging, and the very fact that we do implies that we've done something wrong—something out of step with Nature—because all our needed "anti-aging" processes are already inherent in the body's life-directive to adapt and survive, spare the telomeres (DNA fractions that protects the whole strand). Aging is an important part of life and a human being's life experience. We can age gracefully and without disease. *This* is Nature's plan, and the body's "coin of the realm" of graceful aging is optimal ATP production.

Your cellular membranes are there to preserve the integrity of your cells. Again, we live and die at the cellular level. For cellular nutrition, a person must first eat the proper diet, and also have good digestion. The digestion process breaks down the macro-nutrients: 1) complex carbohydrates to simple sugars, 2) complex proteins to simple proteins and peptides, 3) complex fats to simple fats for cellular utilization. Glycopeptides help the body assimilate the micro-nutrients — vitamins, minerals, trace minerals, humates (humic acid, fulvic acid), and other nutritional factors, and serve as portals in the cell membrane for the cell to receive nutrition.

Next, (skipping over the liver's role in humanizing proteins with a molecule of saturated fat) the cells have to receive their chosen molecules through their membranes.

Today, cell membranes are suffering due to an imbalance of fats, proteins, and detrimental sugars (excessive sucrose, fructose) in the diet — including 1) too much *omega six,* (from overuse of vegetable oils in processed foods when compared to the balance with *omega three* fats), 2) the nutritionally vile inclusion of trans-fats such as partially-hydrogenated oil often used in crackers, cookies, and margarine, 3) not enough of a fatty acid molecule called, *omega three*, 4) heat altered proteins (over cooking, processed foods), 5) improper digestion of proteins due to poor hydrochloric acid production in the stomach, and food combinations that inhibit the protease enzymes, 6) refined sugar (sweets), and also 7) dysbiosis (too many pathogens and not enough beneficial bacteria in the intestines).

Further, many environmental toxins disrupt cellular function and clog the passageways by filling or blocking the cell's glycopeptide receptor sites with useless or toxic molecules. For example, the synthetic sweetner Splenda® is now turning up in municiple water supplies because neither the body nor the municiple purification methods can't break it down. This is creating an environmental concern for fish as well as humans.

Many of the environmental toxins (air pollution), household toxins (cleaners, air fresheners, anti-static dryer sheets, etc.), and food-additive toxins (nitrates, nitrites) serve as oxidation agents that generate *free radicals*§ that damage the delicate cell membranes, and prevent the cells' selectively permeable membrane from functioning properly. As mentioned before, free radicals are electrons that damage cells and are associated with cancer and aging diseases such as cardiovascular disease, failing eyesight, and poor memory.

Environmental Toxicity and Cellular Nutrition. Known universally as "toxicity," the accumulation of air pollutants, food additives, metabolic wastes, household products, pesticides, herbicides, fungicides, prescription drugs, cosmetics, plastics in metal containers (metal cans are lined with plastic), mercury from dental amalgams, prescription drug residues in municipal water can become lodged in the extra-cellular matrix and change the ability of the cells to do the very things they require for life which include:

- Hydrate (receive and discard water)

- Oxygenate (use oxygen for cellular combustion of fuel for energy)

- Receive nutrients

- Have a proper ion exchange system—sodium-potassium pump— electrical conductivity based on pH (acid/alkaline balance which should be slightly alkaline, and proton pump activity)

- Use antioxidant potentials to protect the cells from oxidative stress and the resulting free-radical pathologies such as cancer and autoimmune diseases

- Detoxify and discard metabolic wastes

- Protect themselves from the pathogens (virus, bacteria, myco-bacteria, fungi, parasites, etc.) that Nature sends to help the body clean up the debris in the extracellular matrix (terrain), and eliminate cells that do not fit the body's standard of health

- Reproduce an exact, healthy replica.

This is the reason that the α-glycopeptide molecule is so beneficial to cellular nutrition—where true nutrition really happens. α-Glycopeptides support all these cellular life processes. Coming from rice, α-glycopeptides provide both fuel and nutrients that are made by Nature and are rendered "ready to go" for virtually instant uptake by the cells for energy, communication, and repair.

Very Well Leads to Very Well, Thank You.

Here is a causal chain known as the "we live and die at the cellular level paradigm." It's simple. When the cells have energy, they can do their job, and with a little cooperation, the whole body prospers. Cellular ATP production is a fundamental key to cellular health.

- When the cells have energy, they perform their cellular functions the way Nature designed them to function—**very well**.

- When groups of cells function properly, their tissues perform their functions the way Nature designed them to function—**very well**.

- When all the tissues (organs, glands, bones, muscles) function well, the entire body functions the way that Nature intended—**very well**.

- When the body functions well, the innate self-regulatory mechanisms (vitality, constitution, immune system, metabolism, homeostasis, survival mechanism) function the way Nature designed—**very well**.

- When the innate vitality functions well, symptoms and discomforts drop away and the person lives in a vibrant state of health characterized by excellent energy, strong immunity, clear thinking, creativity, joy, and adaptability. **Very well!**

Very well means just that, being **very well.** Then, when people ask you, "How are you doing today?" If your cells are energized, you can reply "Very well, thank you!" and it will actually be true from a whole body perspective.

Cut To The Chase – Summary #4

We live and die at the cellular level. People with healthy cells (cells that have energy for all their needs) have healthy bodies.

- The only true measure of nutrition is what the cells can accept to perpetuate life processes.

- Practically everyone has impaired digestion which impacts their cellular nutrition

- The toxic environment affects every person and inhibits cellular nutrition.

- Problems with hormones are usually cellular resistance and performance, and not a glandular problem.

- "Alpha" sized molecules are required to nourish the cells.

- α-Glycopeptides (and a-peptides) are embedded in the cell membranes and help escort nutrition into the cell.

- α-Glycopeptides are the premier "anti-aging" supplement.

Just ask a cell, "What do you need for health?" The cell replies: "α-glycopeptides to support the cell membrane, provide nutrition, create ATP, maintain pH, repair DNA, and excrete environmental and metabolic wastes."

Detoxification—A New and Better Paradigm

The brilliance of providing nutrition directly to the mitochondria of the individual cell is this: when the body turns on all its "energy engines", detoxification of the cells, as well as detoxification of the extra-cellular matrix occurs naturally, directed by the body's innate intelligence, and all the body systems cooperate in the detoxification endeavor. This means that the detoxifying process is gentle, hardly noticed by the person, because the body uses all its natural facilities according to its innate processes. Thus deep detoxification is simply "business as usual" and does not have to be a debilitating, exhausting, painful process that occurs when people detoxify without first having good cellular energy.

The Critical Importance of Detoxification. Earlier, we discussed that a common denominator in all chronic degenerative and auto-immune diseases is a lack of cellular energy (ATP). A lack of cellular energy is directly associated with an increase in inflammation because there is not enough energy to fund the detoxification and restoration processes. Pesticides are linked with numerous neuro-degenerative diseases. Toxic chemicals and heavy metals are linked with cancer. Inflammation from toxins affects hormonal behaviors. Without detoxification, the body will die. With reduced detoxification capabilities, the body moves toward a slow death from the resulting disease.

New Rule For Detoxification. The new rule for all dedicated natural health practitioners who help people via detoxification is this: **"First build cellular energy, then detoxify."**

Relying on the body's innate processes, reactivated by α-glycopeptides, is quite different than many of the detoxification protocols that are currently popular in the Natural Health philosophies and practices where chemicals (DMSA, EDTA), and/or herbal chelators, and/or vitamin catalysts are introduced to the body to force detoxification. Such forcing of the detoxification process often stresses the body's ability to remove the toxins (a process called *drainage*), and thus a person may feel tired and achy, and experience skin outbreaks, a runny nose,fever and diarrhea during the "cleansing" process. There is also the risk of Herxheimer[§] reactions where the body has a serious reaction to the detoxification bottleneck and just can't get the freed toxins out of the system.

Glutathione—The Body's Premier Antioxidant. This is some information that delves back into cellular biochemistry, but its conclusion is important to understand.

Glycopeptides help the cells and liver produce *glutathione* – a tripeptide assembled from the amino acids cysteine, l-glutamic acid, glycine and a glutamate molecule. Glutathione is a potent antioxidant that protects the cells and the liver from reactive oxygen species (free radical and peroxide damage). Without glutathione, the cells die because they destroy themselves, or establish errant cellular activities that result in death of the cell, or worse, abnormal cell proliferations.

Your cells' ability to produce their own glutathione is critically important. You can think of glutathione as what the cells use to protect themselves from the combustion of life energy and damage of ion exchange that takes place at the body's atomic level. Thus glutathione could be likened to the lead rods that keep a nuclear reactor from running out of control, melting down, and destroying life.

Further glutathione functions in the nucleus of your cells to protect your RNA and DNA and help facilitate the necessary life processes. Its biological activity is that it can donate a free proton as well as donate electrons, which at the atomic level, is what makes glutathione serve the body as its perfect antioxidant protector and facilitator of its cellular machinery. By donating electrons, glutathione stabilizes free radicals and prevents the cells from being destroyed or becoming cancerous. As an antioxidant, it has the ability to "quench" free radicals without become a free radical itself. Both cirrhosis of the liver and cancers can result from low levels of glutathione. It also maintains Vitamin C and Vitamin E in their active, antioxidant forms.

What this means is that cells make glutathione only if they have available nutrients (peptides) and if they have ATP. Glutathione then protects the cells and causes them to function properly. Peptides plus ATP comprise a significant facet of glutathione production and operation inside the cell and its nucleus.

People with low glutathione levels suffer from more rapid aging, cellular damage, and the struggles to detoxify the body. Thus their life processes get choked down with toxins. Inevitably, low production of ATP results in low glutathione production. Again, low glutathione production results in low energy, toxicity, cellular damage, and disease.

The body makes its own glutathione, and it can't really be supplemented except to take precursor nutrients, because supplemental glutathione has very poor uptake through the human gastro-intestinal tract. By the body's design, glutathione is produced in the cells. Some doctors administer glutathione by injection.

IMPORTANCE OF GLUTATHIONE

The body's primary antioxidant to protect the cells from free radical damage that leads to diseases.

- The body's premier detoxification agent to help eliminate metabolic and environmental toxins.
- Helps vitamin C and vitamin E function.
- Directly detoxifies dangerous chemical toxins and carcinogens.
- Helps with insulin receptor sensitivity (prevents insulin resistance).

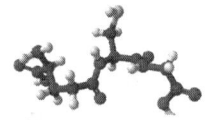

- Essential for the immune system to work properly. Modulates cytokine response and helps proliferate lymphocytes. Enhances the killing activity of cytotoxic T and NK cells, and helps control the immune response so it is not auto-immune.
- Performs DNA synthesis, repairs DNA, helps with prostaglandin synthesis, amino acid transport and enzyme activation.

Every system in the body is affected by glutathione—hepatic, renal, immune, nervous, respiratory, pulmonary, and gastro-intestinal.

To make a glutathione molecule, the cell requires two packets of ATP. As we now know, α-glycopeptides provide the fuel for the cells to make ATP. We also find that the α-glycopeptides provide the amino acids that are part of the glutathione equation.

Detoxification Reactions. Detox reactions are not particularly good (though well-intended) because the toxins can move from the extra-cellular matrix and fat cells into more delicate tissues such as the brain and pituitary gland, and thus disrupt the entire neuro-endocrine system of hormonal feedback loops.

People who have accumulated too many toxins often become "environmentally sensitive". The solution involves detoxification and thus a "catch 22" exists because they are also "pathological detoxifiers," in that they can't handle any detoxification processes without feeling bad and risking further exacerbation of their symptoms. Environmentally sensitive people must detoxify, and blessedly small amounts of α-glycopeptides play a pivotal role in gentle, consistent detoxification in that they help harness the body's innate resources and processes. This makes detoxification easier, more effective, and helps prevent unwanted side effects.

This new model for detoxification is more in line with Natural Law. With proper energy, cells detoxify themselves. With proper energy, the detoxification pathways perform optimally. With optimal detoxification, a person eliminates primary cause of acute illness, chronic degenerative diseases, and unnecessary aging. All three of these health concerns can be the result of a toxic terrain that: 1) invites pathogenic activity-acute illness are a result of pathogens finding a proliferative terrain, 2) inhibits cellular function, blocks hormones and communications, and 3) poor glutathione production that results in rapid aging and cellular damage.

Through intra-cellular communication, cells tell other cells to detoxify, and between them, they exert an influence on the detoxification of the extra-cellular matrix (the collagen and substance between the cells). Toxins that need to move through the body's metabolic pathways—the liver's Cytochrome p450 enzyme processes—can do this better when the gall bladder and kidneys have energy to participate. Thus α-glycopeptides are ushering in a new era of effective, safe detoxification by providing the cells the energy to do what they should have been doing all along—keeping the inner terrain clean and functioning optimally.

For example, no longer must most people force their bodies to release mercury (acquired from dental fillings, vaccinations, certain fish), lead (from the air), chemicals and pesticides (from air and food), and other xenobiotics (cosmetics, household products, industrial pollution) at the expense of feeling bad. Instead, detoxification can occur by the body's directive based on having the energy to detoxify properly. Further, energy reduces the risk of moving toxins to more sensitive tissues or having them alter the epigenetic directives to genes (a primary factor in all the *"no known cause, no known cure"* auto-immune diseases).

Detoxification can better be accomplished by energizing the cells to make ATP. Please note that people with a severe toxic overload or long-term issues with toxicity may require chelation§ agents, glutathione precursor nutrients, increased antioxidants, manual therapies such as colonics and far-infrared saunas, and careful monitoring with the care of a health professional. Every detoxification process can be more effective when the body's innate resources are utilized—and that requires cellular energy and additional ATP.

> "The human body heals itself, and nutrition provides the resources to accomplish the task."
>
> Roger Williams Ph.D. (1971), author of Biochemical Individuality

So why does a person become "toxic" in the first place? Of course we all encounter thousands of toxins daily—in the air, in our water, in our homes, at the mall, in our cars, and in our food. Many of the chemicals and pesticides have an affinity for the fat (adipose) cells – such as the cells of the breasts, and the abdominal extra cellular matrix – so the body will store them there. Why the storage instead of a rapid elimination? Because the cells are not functioning properly, meaning they do not have their detoxification engines running optimally due to a shortage of cellular fuel to make the energy needed for detoxification, e.g. ATP. Thus they do not have adequate glutathione for the task at hand. The body is temporarily overwhelmed with the xenobiotic, acquired chemicals and toxins, so it stashes them in fat cells where they can do minimal harm until such a time the body has energy to detoxify itself.

If you do not have efficient cellular energy production, the body will have a tendency to retain toxins because it simply does not have the cellular fires (energy) to either burn them up or chemically alter them. It's unable to facilitate the needed detoxification processes via the liver, and other eliminative organs—skin, kidneys/bladder, lymphatic system, lungs, gall bladder, and bowels.

As cellular fuel, α-Glycopeptides simply fire up the very processes that the body must have working properly for optimal health performance. Thus the detoxification that is so desperately needed can occur daily, gently, and without the risks of fatigue, aches, and unwanted side effects. α-Glycopeptides say to the body, "Drivers, start your engines and perform the way Nature designed." And Nature's design (your innate blueprint) has an excellent survival factor that has been refined over thousands of years, but we're all having a "run for our money" with the level of global toxicity we encounter daily.

Athletic Enhancement. Here in our discussion on detoxification, let's reiterate our prior comment about the lack of muscle soreness in athletes using α-glycopeptides, because we're really talking about a detoxification process. When muscles work they release a metabolic toxin called *lactic acid* that is associated with muscle soreness. When the cells are energized with plenty of ATP, and there is adequate oxygen intake (exercise), instead of muscles becoming sore with lactic acid, the cells can convert lactic acid to pyruvate, and then use pyruvate to make more ATP energy.

"[Glycopeptides] really helps me recuperate after athletic/sports activities. In fact, it works so well and so fast I recuperate during the sporting event and literally do not experience muscle fatigue *during* or after; Pitching baseball and cycling in my case. I just don't have any after-effects as I've had my entire life before [glycopeptides]."

Dedicated Athlete

As cellular fule, α-glycopeptides help relieve the body's detoxification burden by turning lactic acid, into ATP to support the body's muscle repair processes. Athletes also report that muscle mass improves when dietary peptides (high quality amino acids) are included supplementally in a nutrition program that includes α-glycopeptides.

In working with world class, competitive athletes, I find that they also report quicker muscle recovery time (a function of having ATP energy and good nutrition) as well as increased stamina.

α-Glycopeptides for Detoxification

Here's a recommendation for people starting to take α-glycopeptides. First, know that most people do NOT experience any *noticeable* detoxification side effects, but the process happens behind the scenes, the way Nature intended. But some peoples' cells can be so excited to receive fuel, that their cells instinctively know that they must detoxify so a few people might experience some mild detoxification symptoms.

What are these symptoms? From my clinical cross section of approximately 200 people, eight people expressed some detoxification symptoms that include the following: loose stool (for three days), mild achy joints (passed in two days) mild headache (lasted one day), heart palpitations (lasted one day) and mild malaise (lasted one day). After the detoxification feelings subsided, all eight people were rewarded with much more energy and well-being and then later reported the alleviation of several health concerns. The quick resolution of symptoms were a result of reducing the amount of α-glycopeptides being taken, and then later increasing the amount.

Please understand that the eight people who reported mild detoxification experiences were taking a larger than average amount of α-glycopeptides as part of a therapeutic program. It was easy for them to reduce their dose and support their bodies' corrective efforts, persevere, and then experience the joy of better energy after their "spring cleaning" efforts.

If a person has a toxic burden, that person cannot be healthy until detoxification occurs. With humanity's current state of ignorance regarding exposure to toxins—they are in our air, municipal water, food, clothes, cosmetics, building materials, furniture, household cleaners, lawns, cars, appliances, carpets, etc. Dangerous toxin acquisition occurs daily for everyone. The one universal molecule that stands between you and disease is ATP with it's ability to help your cells produce the body's premier detoxification agent, glutathione.

A rule of thumb might be, if taking α-glycopeptides results in a feeling of detoxification, all you need to do is reduce the amount you are taking and drink more pure water (especially water that is made more efficient by making it "catalyst water§" which results in the water molecules becoming smaller clusters and more able to facilitate the removal of toxins from the cells and out of the body much the way a detergent helps water get grease off a plate). If you are taking other detoxification agents (herbs, glutathione-push products, chelating agents), you should reduce them as the α-glycopeptides are probably making them more effective.

Then, when feeling ready, gently increase the amount of α-glycopeptides to the level you like to take. Generally, if any detoxification reactions occur, they will do so in the first week or two. Some people may have prerequisite improvements to make before their cells are able to properly detoxify. After that, it's smooth sailing on an ocean of greater cellular energy. In my case, after three months on six scoops of α-glycopeptides a day, I had a four-day detox period occur (scratchy throat, night sweats, mild malaise) that did not disrupt my daily schedule and I was thrilled to be getting rid of some deeply-retained toxins.

Cut To The Chase – Summary #5

Effective detoxification processes are critical for health. Detoxification helps reduce the causes of inflammation and chronic degenerative diseases. There are so many new toxins in our air, food, water, and homes, we must have powerfully effective detoxification pathways operating to live in good health.

- Detoxification is an essential and necessary step toward better health.

- Stored toxins are linked to neuro-degenerative, free radical, and chronic diseases.

- ATP is required for detoxification.

- When ATP is low, toxins accumulate.

- When ATP increases, the body can energize its detoxification processes.

- Glutathione is the body's premier antioxidant and detoxification molecule.

- Glutathione protects the cells and their DNA and helps neutralize free radicals.

- α-Glycopeptides increase cellular ATP and helps the cells "clean house."

- If you experience discomfort from enthusiastic detoxification you should reduce the amount of α-glycoepeptides temporarily, increase water intake, and take a more gentle approach to your nutritional improvement process.

People who consistently use α-glycopeptides each day provide their bodies the nutrition and energy to more effectively detoxify, and thus remove various causative factors of disease and rapid aging.

α-Glycopeptides – The Protein Part Of The Health Equation

Okay, I promise to not get into amino acid biochemistry. But I do want to highlight some very important points about α-glycopeptides in human nutrition because they are actually a hundred times more important than the "important sugars" that we've already discussed at length. So α-glycopeptides are ever so much more important than just providing fuel for the mitochondria to make more ATP—as important as that is!

For our perspective, people have had access to *beta* glucans (also called *beta* glycans) from mushroom, yeast, barley, oat bran, paw paw, shark cartilage, and aloe vera plants through derived nutritional supplements for many years. As mentioned before, beta size molecules interact on the cell walls and are not readily received into the inner cells for energy unless enzymes and ATP contribute to the process. *Beta* glycans such as mannose have helped many people with cellular communication issues, but the α-glycopeptides are much more instrumental in building the entire body as well as fueling the cells to make ATP.

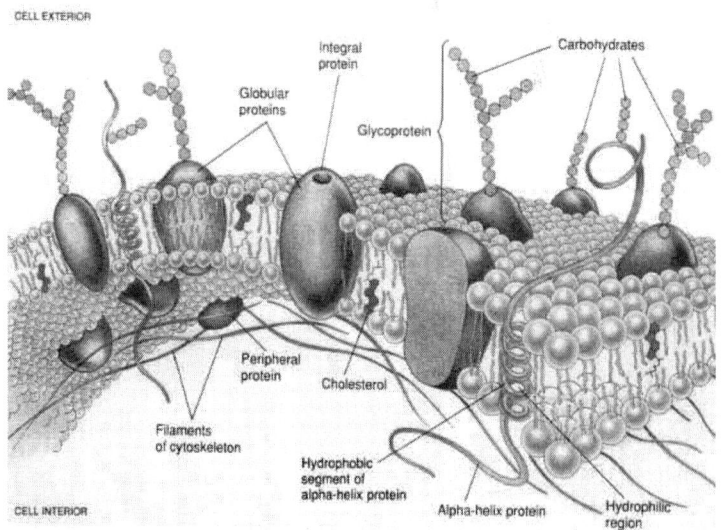

Researchers of glycoproteins have often called glycopeptides, "The most critical molecule for health," and you now understand their enthusiasm as you now know how far reaching and profound these sugar-protein molecules are.

Cellular Signaling. Glycopeptides are the alphabet of cell-to-cell communication, *aka* cell-signaling. Imagine sending a critical, life-saving message but when your message arrives, it's so garbled that the opposite happens, like in the case where the bugle boy sounds "charge!" when the general means, "retreat!"

Our cells have a very detailed and complicated system of communication called *cellular signaling* that governs matters of life and death – our life and death! Cells communicate regarding proper function, cellular activities, responses to the environment, tissue repair, coordination of the immune system regarding pathogens (virus, bacteria, fungus, parasites), responses to hormones, destruction of cancer cells, allergy and inflammatory responses, and many other vital body functions such as cellular differentiation about how a cell is to perform, and also the utilization of stem cells.

Cells talk amongst themselves. Cells talk to the brain and immune system. They place long distance calls, they talk to neighbors over the garden fence, and they talk to themselves as well. Thus there are a wide variety of communication devices similar to a modern day teenager's armamentarium – computer, cell phone, land line phone, walkie-talkie, text message, verbal, written notes, hand signals, attire messages, post-its on the fridge, and so forth.

The communication centers in the body are in and on the cell membranes. And also like the modern teenager, the cell membrane has multiple methods of communication – endocrine, exocrine, molecular, quantum resonance, nitric oxide pathways, and many more.

The primary alphabet of cell-signaling is based on glycoproteins. There are also fats that are important to cell communication known as glycolipids, however glycoproteins (glycopeptides included) are primary communication devices themselves. The "peptide" is embedded in the cell membrane and the "glyco" serves as an antenna.

If there is a shortage of glycopeptides, there can be a communication breakdown that results in confusion, or symptoms of disease. For example, the body needs glycopeptides to communicate with the immune system. Human immune cells known as T-cells (thymus gland derived immune cells that help build the immune system, destroy cancer cells, remember past battles, modify the immune response, and prevent auto-immune responses) are comprised of glycopeptides and rely on a complex signaling network to protect the body from pathogens such as viruses.

When a T-cell encounters a foreign invader, it relays a danger signal to the local cells as well as to distant sensors, incase a quick and decisive response is warranted. These signals cause T-cells to multiply rapidly and send out molecular "distress signals" that attract other immune system molecules (white blood cells) to battle the infection. This whole system of life-saving immune responses is based on glycopeptides.

It is essential to have proper cellular communication. If the message is garbled, the immune system doesn't show up and a cancer cell can proliferate and establish its own blood supply and defenses such as a protein coating. If the message is exaggerated, then the immune system shows up with a cannon when all that was needed was a flyswatter, and this can result in inflammatory damage or auto-immune diseases where the body misinterprets the signals and accidentally attacks a needed body-tissue. Having an abundant supply of α-glycopeptides means that the body has the ability to communicate properly.

Cell Membranes. We've talked about cell membranes being independent and unique organs that have innate intelligence and control which nutrients, messengers and molecules enter and exit the cells. The health of the cell membrane depends upon having high quality dietary fats (the body's requirement for fat is around two tablespoons a day), and an abundant supply of glycopeptides.

Cell membranes are just as important to health as the inner cell and nucleus. More than just a fence holding the cell together, the cell membrane coordinates the inner cellular activities as well as activities in the extra cellular matrix and throughout the body.

Hormones and Neurotransmitters. Many hormones and neurotransmitters are glycopeptides. This makes sense because both hormones and neurotransmitters are vital messengers and facilitators of the body's biochemical processes. Glycopeptides work with other glycopeptides as transmitters and receptors of information.

DNA: Your Body's Operational Manual. The human genetic code contains massive information that the body must be able to open and read. The information written in the code includes the detailed instructions on how to operate the body, how to respond to pathogens, how to be protected from cancer, and how to regenerate tissue. In fact, it's the biochemical operating manual for a healthy life, and it's dependent on Nucleo-peptides, the "peptide" fraction of glycopeptides.

Decode The Genetic Code. Glycopeptides are the molecules that "read" our DNA and then implement the instructions found there. When the body is depleted in glycopeptides due to poor digestion, inhibition of digestion via antacid drugs, and poor quality proteins in the diet, it fails to function properly due to a lack of information.

Balanced Immunity. Immunoglobins are glycoproteins (assemblies of glycopeptides) and α-glycopeptides that regulate the inflammatory processes. Chronic inflammation is linked with so many health issues addressed in the practice of medicine, including auto-immune diseases and most of all, according to medical journals, chronic degenerative diseases such as Alzheimer's, atherosclerosis, rheumatoid arthritis, Crohn's, and arteriosclerosis. Chronic inflammation deranges tissues and results in poor control of body functions.

Chronic inflammation is called the *Tenth Paradigm of Disease*, and is based on a lack of ATP to produce the cell's antioxidants (glutathione peroxidase, superoxide dismutase, catalase) which control the localized inflammatory, free-radical generating reactions.

When there is a dearth of glycopeptides, the immune system can be both over-active (allergies, auto-immune diseases) and under active (susceptible to colds, flu, illnesses). When the cells are unable to effectively signal and communicate, the body becomes errant in its attempts to regulate itself and maintain homeostasis (metabolic balance). Errant behaviors are often handled in Nature by death, but before death comes disease.

Having abundant glycopeptides means that the body's use of the inflammatory response can be reduced and only used when necessary, as Nature as the human genetic code intended.

Artery Integrity. With arterial diseases so rampant, scientists are turning to the role of glycopeptides to understand how the body can maintain the tissue integrity of the blood vessels—arteries, veins, and capillaries. Glycopeptides regulate blood clotting and blood viscosity (how thick or thin the blood is) with the help of the essential fats. They manage the integrity of the arteries – not too brittle, not too pliable. They also reduce inflammation.

The Eighth Paradigm of Disease is called "Ischemic Cardiovascular Disease" and it is the result of a reduction in blood supply to a tissue which results in a loss of tissue function due to the lack of oxygen to make ATP. So here again we see the importance of α-glycopeptides ability to maintain the cellular processes that prevent disease.

Brain Nutrition Must Cross Blood-Brain Barrier

α-Glycopeptides can cross the blood-brain barrier and are used by the body to repair the brain. α-Glycopeptides can help transport other nutritional healers to the brain as well. And α-glycopeptides can be used as brain food boosting the brain's ATP energy. The brain must have abundant ATP to repair and function properly.

With the compelling research that links autism to toxins in the brain such as mercury from vaccinations, pesticides that cross the blood-brain barrier, and disruption of the blood-brain barrier from cell phone radiation. Some medical clinicians cite good results with autism from programs that involve detoxification, and right in the middle of this effort, is glutathione.

Getting more ATP to the brain allows the cells access to the energy they require, and thus can increase glutathione for effective detoxification in addition to providing more of the necessary cell-messenger activity.

Universal Stem Cells. Glycopeptides help the body produce stem cells via the release of innate human growth hormone stored in the pituitary gland. Stem cells are cells that can renew themselves through cellular mitosis (reproduction) and then differentiate into a wide variety of specialized cells. They are the rejuvenators of the body and your body already makes these cells and uses them to heal and repair its tissues, particularly during sleep. Stem cells don't need to be harvested from embryos, your body already makes them, and doing so requires abundant ATP. Both the availability and viability of stem cells are dependent upon having adequate ATP energy production.

Along with what's called *unipotent progenitor cells*, pluripotent stem cells have the ability to repair damaged and malfunctioning tissues. The key to maintaining a youthful body and mind and cultivating longevity is based on the work of stem cells within your body.

Medical research cites that stem cells help the body recover and heal from many severe maladies including: strokes, wounds, missing teeth, baldness (I personally am curious in this regard), learning disorders, neurological diseases, bone marrow malfunctions, spinal cord injuries, glucose metabolic disorders, blindness, deafness, muscle malfunctions, cancers, mitochondrial diseases and thousands of other issues.

Stem cells are universal healers and rejuvenators, and they are available inside your body – when there is adequate ATP energy and the nutritional resources necessary for their work.

Caveat. It's important to understand that we've presented information that shows the importance of cellular ATP production and we've discussed a product that helps the cells make more of their healing and restorative life energy.

However, α-glycopeptides are not a panacea and they are not "the answer" to every health ailment and disease. If you lack in dietary vitamin B12 and have anemia, you need vitamin B-12 to improve your health. α-glycopeptides are not "too good to be true", but are in fact, "too good to not try for yourself." To a person whose health issues are based on a lack of cellular ATP production, α-glycopeptides are a godsend.

There are people who do not notice massive improvements when first they take α-glycopeptides, yet most assuredly α-glycopeptides are there helping behind the scenes, making life work better. The cumulative benefits of supplementing with α-glycopeptides over time demonstrate that little by little, people can nourish their bodies with cell-fuel and cell-signaling molecules and thus provide their bodies a pathway to more optimal function and health.

While a lack of ATP is a root cause of all diseases, there are still other causes that ATP production does not address. For example, if a person has the disease scurvy, the cure is Vitamin C. I repeat such an example to ensure that we know that, while the human ATP energy crisis is a huge cause and common denominator of thousands of symptoms, there is no substitute for obtaining Nature's diet of organic (free of chemicals, pesticides, and additives), raw fruits and vegetables that impart the nutrients for the cells. Increasing ATP production could actually help somewhat, but since the human body does not manufacture its own Vitamin C, the obvious solution is to include foods that contain Vitamin C in the diet.

Cut To The Chase – Summary #6

Cells communicate with glycopeptides. The 'peptide' is embedded in the cell membrane and the 'glyco' is the antenna. This is how the cells coordinate activities and the immune system's responses. It takes ATP energy to communicate and our lives depend upon effective communications.

- Cell membranes communicate throughout the body.
- Glycopeptides are essential for cellular communication.
- Garbled or inadequate messages allow diseases – allergies, cancer, auto-immune.
- ATP funds cell signaling.
- Cell signaling regulates the body's inflammatory response.
- α-Glycopeptides cross the blood/brain barrier to support the brain.
- Stem cells repair and regenerate the body's tissues.
- Stem cell generation and activity requires abundant ATP.

Energy is everything. Clear communication is essential. α-Glycopeptides support both energy and clear communications.

The Eleventh Paradigm of Disease – Lack of Cellular ATP production

In researching α-glycopeptides for this book, I came upon one more topic of interest and an interesting overview. The medical disease paradigms[§] serve as an excellent way for us to develop the overview perspective that transcends the limited scope of this writing and allows us to put this book's perspectives into the practical world.

The medical institution teaches that there are nine paradigms of disease. This means that everything they know about disease falls into nine paradigms or categories. Of course there are many other paradigms needed if medicine is going to meet the challenges of the 21st Century – paradigms that encompass the tenets of bio-energy and the body's innate intelligence, for example. The current challenge for medicine is mastery of the nine paradigms and the inclusion of new paradigms that can better handle the myriad "no known cause, no known cure" diseases that are slipping through the cracks of the medical model – the very diseases that are killing millions of people each year.

It should not come as a surprise that basic nutrition and adherence to Natural Law is the solution to a vast majority of all the facets of all nine paradigms, yet this fact is not universally recognized, particularly since pharmaceutical businesses can't sell a food that helps the body heal itself and thus lose a customer. Here are the nine paradigms, plus one that is being incorporated, and one that is being proposed:

Paradigm #1. Infectious disease. This refers to all the pathogens such as bacteria, mycobacteria, virus, fungus, parasites, and other intelligent organisms that infect the body, particularly when the terrain (pH, and toxins that support pathogens in the extra-cellular matrix) is favorable to their proliferation. Pathogens' actual role in nature is not to hurt people, but to help the body clean up its trash—toxins in the terrain, but sometimes their waste products are very damaging to the body and can cause death. This is why detoxification is so important—

it cleans the terrain so the pathogens are not invited in to do that job.

Medicine treats all pathogens as enemies and has developed powerful weapons to kill them, often with alarming side effects including death, as well as creating superbugs such as antibiotic-resistent *staphylococcus aureus* that eats flesh. When the cells have ample ATP, they maintain a clean terrain and have the energy to defend themselves from pathogens as well as signal the immune system for support.

Paradigm #2. Genetic disease. Refers to illnesses from genetic abnormalities. There are over 4000 diseases that can result from a single gene defect. This includes a new and important interest for medicine—the mitochondrial diseases—because the mitochondria have their own genetics and must maintain and repair their own genetic code. While medicine investigates gene splicing and identification of the genome position of errant genetic expressions, the body has an inherent method to repair and maintain both the nucleus' DNA as well as the mitochondrial DNA. The enzymes and peptides that repair DNA require abundant ATP and basic nutrition at the cellular level. Thus energy (and cellular nutrition) is everything!

Paradigm #3. Nutritional deficiency diseases. This refers to disease such as scurvy, beriberi, iron deficiency anemia, pellagra, and rickets, where the body goes into an overt disease because of a lack of a vitamin or mineral, and cures itself very quickly when the required nutrient is provided dietarily. (Note: pernicious anemia is an autoimmune disease and thus exempt from this paradigm.) Understanding that nutritional deficiencies can lead to overt disease begs the question, "What about suboptimal nutrition, as opposed to overt deficiency, being a factor in all diseases?" The role of nutrition is to provide the body the building blocks of health as well as the fuel for energy—ATP. α-Glycopeptides are 'food for the cells.'

Paradigm #4. Hormone dysfunction diseases. This Forth Paradigm encompasses the entire neuro-endocrine, endocrine and exocrine processes of hormone messengers and the body's ability to regulate its metabolism. As we've discussed, the largest issue here is not the hormone producing glands (thyroid, ovaries, testes, pituitary, etc.), but the ability of the targeted cells to receive the hormone messengers. If the messenger is blocked at the cell membrane by toxins (particularly pesticides), then the message never gets delivered and hormonal mayhem results. The cells require ATP to manage their membranes, induct nutrients through the cell membrane, and handle toxic molecules. Supplementing with α-glycopeptides means that the body's communication system is upgraded. Better communication solves many of the body's regulatory issues.

Paradigm #5. Allergies. This paradigm deals with an immune system disorder of hypersensitivity to what should be harmless substances (food, environment). Here, medicine grapples with allergens, antigens, and antibodies to help desensitize the immune system regarding pollens, foods, and environmental products. Underlying all unnecessary allergic inflammations (hives, asthma, hay fever, eczema) is the role the cells play in alerting the immune system via messenger molecules (glycopeptides, glycolipids, polypeptides), and the need for ATP for proper cell-signaling. α-Glycopeptides can be instrumental in establishing a better balanced immune response.

Allergies can be viewed as: 1) a lack of proper cellular communication, 2) errant communications, 3) a misinterpretation of the communications resulting in an over-exuberant immune response, "I thought you said to drop a blockbuster (bomb), not drop by and pick up a blockbuster movie!" Glycopeptides support proper communication, help avoid errant communications, and thus help ensure that proper messages are sent and received.

Paradigm #6. Autoimmune diseases. This sixth paradigm addresses when the immune system's lock-and-key mechanism becomes errant and the immune system's keys fit the body's own locks – a big mistake in communication and construction of antigen/antibody systems.

Thus if the immune system attacks the thyroid gland, medicine can label it Hashimoto's Disease; if the immune system attacks the joints, it's medically labeled as Rheumatoid Arthritis; if the immune system attacks the intestines, it's called Crohn's Disease by diagnosing physicians, and so forth.

How did the immune system get the cell signals to attack something necessary to the body? One theory is that 'leaky gut syndrome" where particles of food enter the bloodstream before they are properly digested and trigger the immune system's reaction, can be a factor. There are reports of commercial cow milk (but not raw milk) being linked to the autoimmune destruction of the beta cells in the pancreas. Another theory is that the cell-signals from an ailing tissue are improperly constructed or confused. Cells require adequate ATP and good nutrition (α-glycopeptides) to operate its signaling processes accurately. Glycopeptides can help the body reduce inflammation and help repair the intestines.

Paradigm #7. Somatic mutation/selection. This is the cancer paradigm where the cell's DNA becomes damaged by free radicals and the cell starts to behave abnormally, often encouraged by a hormone, with tumor proliferation. Cells require ATP to make their own antioxidants which provide protection from free radicals via glutathione, superoxide dismutase and catalase. Also ATP helps maintain and repair both the cellular and mitochondrial DNA. It also supports the proper utilization of hormones by the cells hormone receptor cites.

With adequate ATP and α-glycopeptides for cell communication, the cell-signaling process can alert the immune system to destroy aberrant cells before they become uppity and establish their own blood supply.

Paradigm #8. Ischemic cardiovascular disease. This paradigm focuses on the reduction in blood supply to a tissue and the resulting low oxygen environment created there. Low oxygen is a favorable terrain for tumors and pathogens, and it also chokes off the cells ability to make the fuel for the production of energy—ATP. Often, lesions in the arteries cause a narrowing of the blood passageways. Lesions are the result of free radical damage that ATP-produced glutathione, as well as other antioxidants should control—if there is adequate ATP and good nutrition. The body's ability to make its own free-radical quenchers (antioxidants) is based on ATP.

Paradigm #9. Amyloid (including prion) diseases. This is the paradigm of mad cow disease (prions) and Alzheimer's, according to the medical literature. Amyloids are large, insoluble, hard-to-manage protein-aggregates that foul up tissue functions and lead to neuro- degenerative diseases. Such proteins can aggregate where there is low-level, chronic inflammation. Thus amyloids are mutated, polymerized protein structures that aberrantly assemble, often in a low ATP environment, or terrain where toxins block the tissues metabolic pathways. Excessive amyloid congestion results in dehydration of the cells which warps the cell membranes and can lead to improper cell-signaling, improper electrical charge, as well as cellular malnutrition.

You can readily see where α-glycopeptides can support the energy and signaling processes to help the body avoid the creation of amyloid structures, as well as provide the necessary energy for the body to resist pathogens using the energy of good health. It's also worth noting that "catalyst water" helps the cells hydrate and flush out toxins.

Possible Paradigm #10. NO/ONOO Cycle Diseases. There is a proposed Tenth Paradigm of Disease that is being considered to join the paradigm club. The letters, pronounced, "No, Oh No!" represent the phrase "Nitric Oxide, Peroxynitrite" in biochemistry terms. Basically, this is the paradigm of localized, chronic, self-perpetuating inflammation based on the cells' inability to make enough antioxidants (glutathione, superoxide dismutase, catalase) to control free radical damage, hence the resulting inflammation. This paradigm overlaps other paradigms, but according to the medical literature, is becoming the repository for Chronic Fatigue Syndrome, Autism, Fibromyalgia,

Post Traumatic Stress Disorder, Amyotrophic Lateral Sclerosis, Migraines, Multiple Sclerosis, Asthma, Parkinsons's, Alzheimer's, Tinnitus, Silicon Implant Syndrome, Wasting Diseases, Irritable Bowel Syndrome, and Multiple Chemical Sensitivities.

The discovery by Dr. Martin Pall at Washington State University that four seemingly unrelated disorders (chronic fatigue syndrome, multiple chemical sensitivity, fibromyalgia, and post-traumatic stress syndrome) all share a common situation where a short-term stressor such as illness, accident, exposure to pesticides or toxins, and emotional upheaval, initiates the nitric oxide/peroxynitrate-mediated inflammation process. But instead of ending soon, it gets locked into a self-feeding, endless cycle resulting in chronic pain and chronic adherence to a disease process. Dr. Pall's solution is to interrupt the disease cycle by supplementing with glutathione precursors and antioxidant nutrients (e.g. n-acetyl cysteine, phosphotidylcholine, trimethylglycine, alpha lipoic acid, glutamine, and taurine.)

The Pall research does not address why this happens to one individual and not another. Could the real reason that the Tenth Paradigm exists be that there is a lack of cellular ATP to produce the body's own innate antioxidants? Seems very likely that this is reason for the cells not having the required antioxidants to control the stress-response inflammatory process — they lack Nature's foods and ATP.

Soapbox Commentary. All the human disease paradigms directly lead back to a lack of: 1) basic nutrition, 2) proper digestion, 3) effective assimilation -- rendering of molecules to support ATP production, and 4) having cell-signaling molecules. Basic nutrition is the one area that modern medicine chooses to ignore as inconsequential. This is why millions of people are choosing to shun toxic drugs and dangerous, often unnecessary surgeries and return to the fundamental Law of Life – *energy is everything*, and energy comes from wholesome, unadulterated nutrition.

This Author's Proposed Paradigm #11. Lack of Adequate Cellular Production of ATP. As long as the human mind is creating paradigms to try to grapple with the concept of diseases, I feel compelled to propose an eleventh paradigm as the "mother of all other paradigms." This mother paradigm is the lack of ATP production at the cellular level. We've learned in this book that the cells need oxygen, nutrients and fuel to make ATP. Thus we know that our cellular health depends upon: 1) exercise, 2) whole foods straight from Nature, 3) ability to detoxify, 4) ability to signal the immune system, and 5) ability to repair. Because of our current cultural productivity to: 1) avoid exercise, 2) grow *quantity* instead of *quality* foods, 3) create vast environmental toxicity, and 4) eat junk food quickly, everyone alive is engaged, at some level, with the inhibition of the mitochondrial ATP manufacturing processes. Inevitably, this is the start of every disease, and why, in my humble opinion, everyone can benefit from supplementing α-glycopeptides.

Today more than ever, our bodies can use a boost of fuel to prime the ATP production process. Nutritional α-glycopeptides are doing just that. As demonstrated in this "paradigm" discussion, nutritional α-glycopeptides are the universal molecule to support the cells to make the ATP required for optimal health.

Summary

Here we are near the end of this discourse on nutritional α-glycopeptides and some of the possible benefits with supplementation. Nutritional enhancement with α-glycopeptides can support your body's innate quest to provide you with the most optimal health possible. To summarize the key points we've covered, you can test yourself here to see if I've communicated effectively, here is a list of the salient points:

1. Nutritional α-glycopeptides are uniquely and proprietarily processed, whole body, cellular support food molecules that serve: 1) the mitochondrial production of ATP energy, 2) cell membrane processes including cell-signaling, induction of nutriments, and egress of toxins, 3) whole body nutritional enhancement of vitamins, minerals, antioxidants, healing sugars, and nucleo-proteins.

2. The α-glycopeptides of this book's discussion are processed from special, super-strains of pollutant-free, cross-pollinated rice one with added spirulina, one with "medical rice"- that when hydnolyzed, render the proprietary α-glycopeptides that support human nutritional health.

3. To be readily available to the cells, nutritional molecules must be 'alpha' sized – e.g. very, very tiny. Larger molecules require disassembly by enzymes (work), or the cells cannot use them for their internal processes. The α-glycopeptides discussed here are proprietarily reduced to their natural alpha size.

4. People today, in the opinion of this author, are grossly deficient in the production of ATP from the modern-day diet. This is the fundamental basis of the human energy crisis so rampant today, and a cause behind practically all diseases and aging processes.

5. α-Glycopeptides support mitochondrial production of ATP, the energy of life. The body uses ATP for every activity (work) that keeps us alive and in the best of health possible.

6. α-Glycopeptides support cell-signaling, both with the components of the cell-signaling alphabet itself, as well as the membrane production and implementation of cell signals that organize collective tissue functions and maintain the extracellular terrain. Thus they play a vital role in proper immune responses to pathogens, allergens, and aberrant cells, as well as detoxification and health maintenance.

7. The mitochondria organelles, of which there are thousands in a single cell, have their own DNA and require ATP to repair and maintain themselves in excellent health. When the mitochondria are healthy, the body does not get the dreaded mitochondrial diseases. If the mitochondrial DNA becomes damaged, then the cell cannot function normally.

8. Supplying the mitochondria with their perfect fuel (the *glyco* fraction of α-glycopeptides) for production of ATP is "ground zero" for allowing the body to have the opportunity to correct symptom expressions that are based on a lack of cellular energy.

9. Adequate ATP and the resulting mitochondrial production of antioxidants protects cells from aging, degeneration, and aberrant behaviors. Thus the cells are able to replicate themselves with good integrity based on their original, youthful blueprint.

10. ATP production is equated with maintaining youthfulness, the ability of the body to self-repair, and prevention of aging diseases.

11. α-Glycopeptides support athletic endeavors by helping the muscles recover and repair, as well as helping the body process lactic acid into more energy instead of soreness.

12. The peptide fraction of α-glycopeptides, is by far, more important to health than the valuable and necessary *glyco* fraction that serves the body's ATP production and cell signals because, in human nutrition, the nucleo-proteins (*alpha* sized amino acids)

are used for cellular communication, hormone production, tissue repair, antibodies that support human immunity, and thousands of other life-support functions such as DNA repair.

13. The goal of digestion is to render alpha-sized sugars, proteins and fats because nutrition is only as good as what the cells can assimilate and use for life processes.

14. α-Glycopeptides help with memory and brain function via the increased production of ATP, and they enhance the body's innate detoxification processes.

15. Increasing ATP production to activate the body's innate detoxification processes increases glutathione production with the cells, and is according to this author, a new paradigm for every detoxification program, and a major breakthrough in how human beings can protect their health in the 21st Century's terribly polluted environment.

16. α-Glycopeptides support the body's anti-inflammatory processes so that necessary inflammations (e.g. injuries, wounds) can resolve quickly without becoming chronic. Long term, low level inflammations cause tissue deterioration, poor tissue function, and lead to various chronic degenerative diseases and auto-immune diseases. α-Glycopeptides provide antioxidants as well as boost the body's ability to make its own, nascent antioxidants. They also provide the molecules for the cell membranes to communicate with the immune system effectively so that the cells can help control the immune system's inflammatory response.

17. The author proposes an 11th Paradigm of Disease – the lack of cellular production of ATP—as a root cause of medicine's other disease paradigms and the 'mother of all disease paradigms.'

18. There are an overwhelming multitude of testimonials about improved energy, For many people, cellular energy translates to physical energy. Improved energy is a typical and frequent experience of people supplementing their diets with α-glycopeptides.

19. Energy is everything. Everything is energy.

Now, we've come full circle. Hopefully out of this discussion you are ready to try some α-glycopeptides for yourself. You can do that by contacting the person who shared this information (see the box at the end of this book for that purpose.) Best wishes in your natural health endeavors!

Glossary Of Terms

Active Transport – In cell biology, energy inside the cell membrane is expended to open a portal through the cell membrane so that needed nutrients such as sodium, potassium, glucose (sugars) and peptides (proteins) can pass into the cell for the cell's health and optimal function. The cell also uses Active Transport to expel toxins and wastes from inside the cell. The Active Transport system requires and expends energy. A system called "Passive Transport" does not require an energy expenditure to pass something through the cell membrane because it uses osmosis or laws of permeability. Thus if the Active Transport system is used, there is a cost to the body measured in energy.

Alpha Glycan – The term "glycan" refers to polysaccharides (a chain of carbohydrate molecules) and the term "alpha" refers to the tiny molecular size that can pass through the membrane and be used inside the cell. Glycans are often associated with polypeptides (proteins) that serve the cells with the building blocks of health. Alpha glycans are able to quickly cross cellular membranes and be received by the cells as sustenance. The mitochondria and other cellular organelles (golgi bodies) use glycans in the alpha size to make molecules that support life – energy and structure.

Anthocyanin – Plant pigment factors, flavanoids that have tremendous antioxidant and radical scavenging effects that protects cells from oxidative damage (free radicals) and reduce risk of cardiovascular diseases and cancer. Dietary intake of anthocyanins help inhibit the development of cancer, obesity, and diabetes as well as help contain inflammatory mechanisms.

ATP – Abbreviation for adenosine triphosphate. An ester of adenosine and triphosphoric acid, $C_{10}H_{12}N_5O_4H_4P_3O_9$, formed aerobically by the reaction of ADP and an orthophosphate during oxidation, or by the interaction of ADP and phosphocreatine or certain other substrates, and serving as a source of energy for physiological reactions, especially muscle contractions. In simple terms, ATP is the body's chemical life energy, the currency the body uses to accomplish its life-processes.

Catabolism – The breaking down of complex molecules into smaller molecules in pursuit of energy. Proteins are broken down into amino acids. Fats are broken down into lipids. Carbohydrates are broken down into simple sugars. This process results in heat, energy, and waste products (which can often be rendered into cellular energy if there is adequate ATP to conduct that recovery process.) Catabolism is the opposite of "anabolism" which is a building up of molecules.

Catalyst Water – Water that has a catalyst micelle added that results in the water becoming "wetter", a better solvent, and better utilized in the body for nutrient absorption and toxin removal. Helps scavenge free radicals and raises alkalinity. The Enzacta corporation markets a catalyst water concentrate called "Alpha Energy".

Catch-22 – A book by Joseph Heller. This is a reference to a bureaucratic catch, which embodies multiple illogical and paradoxical reasoning. Generally refers to a situation where there is always an exception to any rule. For example, to be dismissed from combat, a soldier must be deemed crazy, but if the soldier wants to preserve his or her life and leave combat duty, then he is not really crazy.

Cavitation – A hole in the bone, often where a tooth has previously been extracted. Cavitations can occur in any bone in the body, but are most frequently found in the jawbones. The most common site is the wisdom tooth area. It can store mercury from silver amalgam dental fillings as well as bacterial wastes.

Cell-signaling – Human cells have a complex communication system that coordinates activities between various cells. Cells have innate intelligence and the ability to perceive and respond to their environment. Cell-signaling is the basis of proper immune response, tissue repair, detoxification, and homeostatic function. Faulty cell-signaling can result in auto-immune diseases, cancer, and diabetes.

Chelation – Derived from the Greek word "chele", meaning "claw". Chemical definition: One substance binds to another substance. The "grabbing substance" is called the "chelating substance." The grabbed substance is called the "chelated substance." Technically, chelation firmly binds a metal ion with an organic molecule (ligand) to form a ring structure. The resulting ring structure protects the mineral from entering into unwanted chemical reactions. A chelated mineral that can be utilized by the body is one that has been bonded to two or more amino acids from hydrolyzed protein. A mineral in this chelated state allows easy passage through the intestinal wall into the blood stream, which results in increased metabolism of that mineral. In detoxification, chelation refers to grabbing a toxic molecule and binding it into a form that can more easily be excreted from the body.

Ch'i – Also spelled "Qi." In Traditional Chinese Medicine, it refers to the life force or the stored essential energy for life. The kidneys are the repository of a specific kind of ch'i. In other contexts it is called *élan vital*, and *prana*. More specifically, it is the flow of energy through and around the living body that links the body and environment into a cohesive functioning unit. Congestion in the flow of ch'i results in disease and pain. Circulation of ch'i is representative of good health and longevity.

Dysbiosis – The condition of having microbial imbalances within the body, especially within the gastro-intestinal tract. This particularly refers to the loss of the body's innate, colostrum-provided, genetically personalized strains of beneficial bacteria that support digestion and absorption of nutrients, as well as plays a primary role in helping the immune system. The largest source of damage to the intestinal flora, resulting in dysbiosis, is the use of antibiotic drugs. Dysbiosis is linked with allergies, chronic inflammation, and autoimmune diseases.

Endosperm – The tissue produced by flowering plants to encase and nourish the seed at the time of fertilization. The endosperm contains nutritional starches (polysaccharides), proteins (polypeptides), and essential fats. Germane to this book, the endosperm refers to the part of the rice seed that humans eat for nutrition.

Enzacta Corporation – The company that researches, procures, processes, and distributes the Alpha PXP (*polysaccharide/polypeptide*) products as well as other products including humates, catalyst water, nutritional beverages, skin care, and Vitamin B12.

Epigenetic – Changes in gene functions that do not involve changes in DNA sequences. Affected by food, subtle energies (bio-energy), herbs, thoughts, feelings, chemicals, drugs, and environment. It's the material around the DNA strands that activates certain gene-expressions (for better or worse) based on both internal and external influences.

Free Radical – An atom or group of atoms that have at least one unpaired electron and is therefore unstable and highly reactive. In animal tissues, free radicals can damage cells and are believed to accelerate the progression of cancer, cardiovascular disease, and age-related diseases.

Gluten – A protein substance that remains when starch is removed from cereal grains; gives cohesiveness to dough. For many people, gluten is highly allergenic and causes intestinal inflammation and other inflammatory diseases.

Glycolipid – A lipid (fat) with a carbohydrate (sugar) molecule attached. In human biology, glycolipids provide energy and genetic markers (cellular identity) for cellular recognition by the immune system.

Glyconutrient – A marketer-coined word that has now entered common public usage. In public usage, it refers to the eight important (but not really "essential") sugars required by the body for optimal health. Glyco means sugar. Beyond providing fuel, glyconutrients are essential for the body to heal and repair, as well as maintain optimal metabolic functions.

Glycopeptide – Similar to a glycoprotein, but has smaller proteins (amino acid chains) thus is more "cell-ready."

Glycoprotein – A sugar molecule attached to a protein molecule. It plays essential roles in the body, especially for the immune system.

Herxheimer Reaction – Occurs when large quantities of toxins are released into the body as pathogens die (bacteria, yeast, fungus, parasites) from a remedial therapy, or heavy metals are released from the adipose cells into the lymphatic system. The death of the pathogen and the associated release of endotoxins occurs faster than the body can remove the toxins via the kidneys and liver/gallblader. This can result in the body responding with fever, chills, headache, myalgia (muscle pain), and exacerbation of skin lesions. The intensity of the reaction reflects the intensity of inflammation present. The concept of Herxheimer reactions became popular with people doing candida cleanses where the killing of the yeast-fungus released the metabolic and environmental wastes (heavy metals) within the candida cells into the bloodstream and lymphatics.

Humanization – The liver's process of changing "foriegn" molecules into "self" molecules by adjusting the molecular structure, often by adding a molecule of saturated fat. The immune system should not react to "self" molecules but will react to "non-self" molecules.

Hydrolyzation – To cause a substance to split into component parts by the addition of water. This scientific process may also involve enzymes and pressure.

Iatrogenic – Injury, disease or death induced inadvertently by a physician or surgeon, or by medical treatment or diagnostic procedures. Refers to the massive deaths (over 780,000 a year in the United States according to researcher Dr. Gary Null) resulting mostly from drug prescriptions and drug interactions, as well as surgeries.

Ketone – Compounds that contains a carbonyl group attached to a carbon in a chain. Used as analgesics, anti-inflammatories, expectorants, and stimulants. The body can use ketones in the Krebs Cycle to render ATP when adequate carbohydrates are not available.

Ketosis – Having elevated levels of ketones in the blood. The metabolic state where fats are broken down in a process called lipolysis to render ketones for energy.

Leptin – (Greek, *leptos* meaning thin) is a protein-hormone that plays a key role in regulating energy intake and expenditure, as well as appetite and metabolism. It is one of the most important adipose-derived (fat cell) hormones.

Mitochondrion (singular), **Mitochondria** (pleural) – inside most cells, there are organelles known as "mitochondria" that are often referred to as "cellular power plants" because they generate most of the cell's adenosine triphosphate (ATP) which is the source of the body's chemical energy. Mitochondria are also involved in cellular communication (signaling) where the cell's innate intelligence is able to perceive changes in its environment and direct responses such as tissue repair, immunological actions, and homeostasis. When the mitochondria cannot perform correctly (often due to a lack of raw materials to generate energy), diseases such as diabetes, cancer, and auto-immune diseases often occur.

Nanotechnology, Shortened to "**nanotech**", is the study of the controlling of matter on an atomic and molecular scale. Generally nanotechnology deals with structures of the size 100 nanometers or smaller in at least one dimension, and involves developing materials or devices within that size. A size of one-billionth of a unit of measure. Nanotechnology is very diverse, ranging from extensions of conventional device physics to completely new approaches based upon molecular self-assembly, from developing new materials with dimensions on the nanoscale to investigating whether we can directly control matter on the atomic scale. A "two-edged sword" that can be used for good or ill depending upon adherence to the Laws of Nature.

Panacea – A remedy for all disease or ills, a cure-all.

Paradigm – A philosophical and theoretical framework of a scientific school or discipline within which theories, laws, and generalizations and the experiments performed in support of them are formulated; broadly: a philosophical or theoretical framework of any kind. More simply, it refers to a way of doing things.

Polypeptide – Refers to a linkage of several (*poly* means "many") simple proteins (peptides) into a chain that the body can access for many life processes including nucleoproteins (tiny protein structures used inside the cell and nucleus), as well as tissue structure, hormones, immune system cells, and cellular energy processes.

Polysaccharide – Refers to carbohydrate structures ($C_6H_{10}O_5$ – comprised of carbon, hydrogen and oxygen) that are linked together as repeating units. Poly means "many" and saccharide means "carbohydrate." Polysaccharides play an important role as part of the optimal fuel for the cell to create energy. They also play a major role in the workings of the immune system, reproductive system, elimination of pathogens, blood clotting, and body development.

Probiotic – According to the currently adopted definition by FAO/WHO, probiotics are, "Live microorganisms which when administered in adequate amounts confer a health benefit on the host". Lactic acidbacteria and bifidobacteria are the most common types of microbes used, but certain yeasts and bacilli may also be helpful. Probiotics are commonly consumed as part of fermented foods with specially added active live cultures such as in raw milk yogurt, kefir, or as dietary supplements.

Proton Pump – A cell membrane protein that is capable of moving protons across the cell membrane—both the cell wall and the mitochondrial membrane. In cell respiration, the pumps grab protons from the space enclosed by the two membranes and moves it across the membrane. The confined protons create a difference in both pH and electric charge and acts as a kind of battery or reservoir of stored energy for the cell. The inner cell membrane functions in a similar way to a dam in a river. It blocks protons from drifting back inside the membrane. The pumping action requires work (ATP-energy). The process is just like charging a battery (storing potential energy). The proton pump does not create but stores energy for the cells to use to allow nutrients to pass into the cell and waste products to depart the cell.

Pyruvate – Pyruvate is the end product of glycolysis. It is converted into Acetyl-CoA which enters the Krebs cycle when there is sufficient oxygen available. When the oxygen is insufficient, pyruvate is broken down anaerobically, creating lactate in animals that can cause causes muscle soreness, and creates ethanol in plants.

Symptoms – The body's perfect expression of the result of something not working correctly. The body's decision to do the best it can with what it has to work with. *Acute symptoms* (fever, diarrhea, vomiting, skin eruptions, coughs, etc.) are the body's expressions of its innate healing vitality attempting to correct something, or eliminate toxins and pathogens. Chronic symptoms are most often the result of a lack of energy (ATP) at the cellular level that can result in either a weak or overactive immune system. Note: symptoms are the body's communication to help it "correct the cause" of the symptom, not a request to sweep the symptom under the carpet with a suppressive drug (though a drug may be required to reduce tissue damage while the body endeavors to correct the cause.)

Telomeres – Formerly known as "junk DNA," a region of DNA located on the ends of chromosomes that protect the genetic code from degeneration. DNA strands can lose their telomeres when they reproduce – like shoestrings can lose their plastic tips – resulting in an unraveling of the DNA and loss of cellular identity.

Ubiquinol – The active, bioavailable form of Co Enzyme Q-10. CoQ10 plays a key role in producing energy in the mitochondria, the part of the cell responsible for the production of energy in the form of ATP.

Vital Force – Within each cell, within each person's body, is an innate vitality with the life-directive to adapt and survive. It is the body's self-regulatory mechanism. It is the innate wisdom that moves to dispel that which disrupts the body's performance.

Xenobiotic – A completely synthetic chemical compound, which does not naturally occur on earth, and is believed to be resistant to environmental degradation. Loosely refers to all chemicals that do not belong in the human body. This includes all synthetic drugs and hormones, food additives, preservatives, pesticides, fungicides, herbicides, chemicals, plastics, and heavy metals, etc.

Acknowledgements & Thank Yous

Thank you to my wife, Janine, without whose help the path would be insurmountably steep.

Thank you to David Block, Sales Director of Enzacta, Int'l, for his encouragement so this research report can help support the mission of having millions of people experience that "ATP Feeling" of inner strength that comes from improving cellular nutrition.

Thank you to Don Ginn, who suggested that I write on this subject, and who shared his insights and research on how glycopeptides can affect miraculous results in people on the brink of impaired lives due to chronic degenerative issues.

Thank you to Judy Woodward, who meticulously improved the communication potentials of the text and helped clean up the idiosyncrasies of my writings.

Thank you to Joanne McRae Schultz, who voluntarily edited the text and helped me avoid the chagrin of the ever lurking and ubiquitous typo.

Thank you to those who shared an insight or two: Bridget Bagley, Kevin Hentges, Dick Herrboldt, Patty Morris, David Segovia, Jesus Zarzar.

Special thanks to Dr. Doug Gabbert who reviewed the content.

Special thanks to Dr. Luis Romero and Dr. Dan Clark for sharing knowledge from the medical perspective.

And thank you for reading this book. May you also experience the benefits of cellular nutrition.

About the Author
Dr. Jack Tips, N.D., Ph.D. ,C.Hom., C.C.N., www.jacktips.com

by Robert Imbriale, Personal Friend

I first met Dr. Jack Tips in the summer of 1996 while attending Life Mastery University in Kona, Hawaii—a program hosted by world-renowned success coach, Anthony Robbins. At the time, what I did not know was that Dr. Tips was a renowned expert in nutrition, herbology, homeopathy, detoxification, and the natural laws that govern health and healing; and that he was personally chosen by Tony Robbins to present his groundbreaking material to a standing ovation of more than 1,500 people. Tony introduced Jack as a "nutritional genius." I now know that was because of Jack's clear insights that can peer through the smokescreen of nutritional confusion and bring a common sense clarity to the seemingly complex issues that trouble the "experts."

Following his eye-opening presentation, I made my way through the crowd to meet him in person. I purchased a copy of his book, "*Your Liver, Your Lifeline.*" About a year later, I contacted him again over the Internet to see if he had any new books available. A month later, during his travels, he and I had the opportunity to spend the afternoon together while he was changing planes in Chicago and it was then that I got to know him much better.

Jack Tips is a man with a great heart for people—all people. His life is dedicated to helping people lead healthy lives without the need for invasive procedures and harmful chemicals. But Dr. Tips has a much bigger mission in life. He is committed to finding a better way to feed the world's hungry populations with healthful, tasty, and affordable foods that truly nourish the cells, as well as bring the message of health to the overfed-but-undernourished people subsisting on denatured foods.

In the course of his many and varied studies, he earned an undergrad-

THE HEALING POWER WITHIN

uate degree from the University of Texas, and a doctorate degree in Nutrition Science from the Roger Williams School of Nutrition Science. He is licensed as a Dietician/Nutritionist in New York. He is certified in classical homeopathy by the Hahnemann Academy of North America; in Naturopathy by the American Naturopathic Medical Association; in Clinical Nutrition by the prestigious International & American Associations of Clinical Nutritionists.

Dr. Tips has studied with many of the world's most renowned natural health leaders, including: Dr. Herbert Shelton, Dr. Bernard Jensen, Stanley Burroughs, Dr. Paul Eck, Dr. Alan Beardall, Dr. Wilhelm Langreder, Dr. Francisco Eizayaga, Dr. Robin Murphy, and served as a protégé of Dr. A.S. Wheelwright, one of the great herbalists of the 20th Century.

In 1984, he began a clinical practice based on a three-tiered approach to health: classical homeopathy to stimulate vitality, systemic herbology to support specific tissues, and clinical nutrition for metabolic balance. He also lectures at a variety of naturopathic and medical schools around the world on natural healing and the natural laws of health.

When not traveling the world to lecture, learn, and meet people, he resides with his wife and extended family in Austin, Texas. You can reach him by phone at 512.328.3996 and by email at apple-a-day@austin.rr.com.

Dr. Tips is so much more than an expert in natural health, he's a man with a passion for life and a vision of how to make life more enjoyable – naturally! He seeks to support eco-developments as well as and a quest that all life on Earth enjoy true health, potable water, fresh air, wholesome nutrition, and personal freedom. I trust you will enjoy this time and book and will take its advice to heart.

123

Apple-A-Day Press – A Few Selections
Natural Healing At Your Fingertips

3736 Bee Caves Road, Suite 1, Box 174, Austin, Texas 78746
Phone: 512.328.3996 Fax: 512.330-0704

www.apple-a-day-press.com
Email: apple-a-day@austin.rr.com

Toll Free Order Line (24-hours secure): 877.442.7753

Welcome to Apple-A-Day Press – your resource for natural health information featuring the insights of Dr. Jack Tips. Here you'll find some of the most informative books and fascinating training programs available in the world today! Since 1984, Apple-A-Day Press has published books and natural health courses that have helped hundreds of thousands of people improve their health. Here you will find information congruent with the "Natural Laws of Life and Healing from the causative perspective." Any one of these books can change your life! Best wishes in your health endeavors!

- ***The Pro-Vita! Plan for Optimal Nutrition*** by Dr. Jack Tips is one of the most significant nutrition books of the 20th Century, updated in 2004 and totally applicable today. An absolute 'must read' for anyone wanting the official operating manual for the care and feeding off the human body featuring how to build health, prevent disease, and be biologically youthful—the way Nature intended. Jam-packed with profound nutritional insights to improves your nutritional health via simple, delicious, and energizing foods! ISBN 0929167058, 376 pages, index.

- ***The Weight Is Over*** by Dr. Jack Tips. A sequel to the Pro-Vita! Plan with a focus on weight loss, this book explains why people have trouble with weight issues and how simple dietary adjustments play a critical role in health maintenance. Advertised on TV for two years, this book has helped thousands improve their nutritional health. Features the 12 Optimal Food Factors by which you can judge every food and every diet. Truly empowering information, easy to read, hundreds of illustrations. ISBN 092916721X, 300 pages.

- **Passion Play** by Dr. Jack Tips. If ever a book could inspire changes in your life—improve your health, wealth, and relationships; and help you become congruent with your purpose in life—this is the one! Here you'll discover a new perspective on how to play the game of life via the five elemental spheres of influence that govern your success, purpose, and joy. Features insights on the Native American Mirror Technique guaranteed to increase your personal power for optimal results. A milestone discourse on the laws of manifestation, self-realization, performance and success. ISBN 0929167201, 333 pages.

- **Conquer Candida** – *Restore Your Immune System* by Dr. Jack Tips. Written during the candida pandemic of the 1980's, this book was the first to reveal that candida is not the enemy and thus became prophetic by revealing the deeper philosophies of natural health and true healing. With modern day discoveries regarding inflammatory and auto-immune processes, this material is a primer for how to maintain the integrity of your immune system. ISBN 0929167007, 163 pages.

- **Breast Health** by Dr. Jack Tips. From the natural health perspective, there are clear reasons why breast cancer is pandemic. Knowing this means you can protect your health. A featured publication for National Breast Health week, this manuscript teaches simple methods to ensure that the breast tissue stays healthy. Shows the relationship between breast health and PMS and gynecological concerns. Teaches the breast massage lymphatic drainage technique necessary for proper hormonal balance. 56 pages, illustrations.

- *Next Step to Greater Energy* by Dr. Jack Tips. Are your "little addictions" a sign of metabolic imbalance? Explore your body's energy glands (thyroid, adrenals) and bio-energy as well as neurotransmitter and biochemical balance. Stopping smoking is a primary focus of this information. A prequel to Passion Play, this information explores personal health freedom for fuller spiritual expression. Out Of Print. Available only as a web download or as a mailed pdf file. ISBN 092916704X, 210 pages.

- *Your Liver—Your Lifeline (The Healing Triad)* by Dr. Jack Tips. Learn how your most important organ is a key part of your immune system as well as how to detoxify your entire body by building your inherent liver function. Featured at Anthony Robbins' Life Mastery University, this book discusses the liver's multiple bio-forces and Doc Wheelwright's miraculous herbal discoveries. A must read for people with liver concerns. ISBN 0929167066, 150 pages.

- *New Dimensions In Herbal Healing* by Dr. Jack Tips. Finally! A book that explains the pioneering, bio-energetic, herbal research of one of the 20th century's great healers—A.S. Doc Wheelwright. Learn about the most effective herbal Healing System available today and how herbs are the true medicine for the challenges of living in the 21st Century. Focuses on the Systemic Bio-Commands – a method that promotes healing directives. Features protocols for the Kidneys, Thyroid, Brain Building, Heart Building, A.D.H.D., Liver, Cleansing, Female Hormones, and Lungs. ISBN 0929167236, 110 pages.

- *Blood Chemistry & Clinical Nutrition* by Jack Tips. Clinically effective, nutritional insights from the routine "auto-chem" (SMAC-26/CBC lab report).For the clinical nutritionist, this desk reference examines each blood test value from the SMAC-26/CBC lab test for its nutritional health implications and provides Systemic herbal protocols for correcting imbalances. Includes optimal values, pathologies, clinical notes, cross-references, protocols and valuable insights from other clinicians. An essential tool for the practicing health professional. 123 pages, ISBN 0-929167-07-4 $44.95

- ***Dragon Rising: Clinician's Guide to the Systemic Chinese Constitutional Formulas*** by Tena Scarber and Jack Tips. In the late 1980's, Doc Wheelwright created the Systemic Chinese Five-Element herbal formulas to address people's constitutional and emotional states. Based upon historic Chinese and Japanese traditions, he perfected the bio-energetic impact of time-honored, constitutional herbology and opened up a deeper dimension to herbal healing. This book, a collaborative effort by Jack Tips and Tena Scarber (Acupuncturist), first teaches the Chinese Five-Element foundation and progresses into the unique Wheelwright perspective of bio-energetic correction of fundamental imbalances to create a system of clinical applications to improve the impact of any herbal/nutrition program. ISBN #0929167295, 150 pages.

www.apple-a-day-press.com

Index

Symbols

A

B

W

X

Y

Z

**For more information about supplementation with
α-glycopeptides (polysaccharide/polypeptides), please contact:**